This Book Could Save Your Child's Life

OUR DAUGHTER'S DYING WISH
TO SHARE HER DIARY
AND SAVE LIVES FROM DRUGS

Her Words from Beyond the Grave

Victoria's Voice

DAVID AND JACKIE SIEGEL
"The Queen of Versailles"

Featuring the diary of Victoria "Rikki" Siegel

MOMOSA PUBLISHING

Cover design by Nicole Miranda and Leanne Coppola

Photos on pages 228 to 261 from DEA.gov.

Library of Congress control number 2018961870

ISBN 978–1–7323016–1–0

2 4 6 8 10 9 7 5 3 paperback

Victoria's Voice

To the memory of Victoria

Our Hope

Our daughter's legacy is that because of her death,
many more people will live.

—*David and Jackie Siegel*

Contents

Foreword

by Robert Shapiro,
attorney and entrepreneur

Victoria Siegel was just 18 when she lost her life. And she did so because of the prescription drug culture here in America. If you feel bad, take a pill and feel better. It's fast, and it works. But it's short term. You cannot live a life that is driven by drugs: a life of ever-decreasing highs and ever-increasing levels of pain and suffering.

Victoria's Voice is a book like no other. It tracks the real-life breakdown of a young girl caught up in the cycle of prescription medications, street drugs, and all of their terrible side effects. Reading her story brought tears to my eyes because I lost my son Brent to an accidental drug overdose (amphetamines and MDMA) in 2005.

Since then I founded the Brent Shapiro Foundation to raise awareness about the massive problem this country has with psychoactive drugs. I also opened Pickford Lofts, a place where recovering addicts can live until they are strong enough to re-enter the outside world.

Like myself, my good friends David and Jackie Siegel also decided that their tragedy should serve as a way of helping others. They have respected their daughter's wishes in life and published her diary to shed some light on the darkness of addiction. It was brave of them to open the door to the most terrible episode in their lives.
They did so because for every life they save, the loss of their daughter becomes slightly less meaningless and perhaps just a bit more bearable.

Help your kids understand the dangers that are out there and give them this book. It really gets the message home like no other book about addiction I have ever read. Give them the power of knowledge so they can weigh the pros and cons and take control before drugs get a chance to control them.

Introduction
by Jackie Siegel

Losing my daughter Victoria "Rikki" Siegel when she was just 18 years old was the most devastating event in my life. When Victoria passed away on June 6, 2015, my world changed forever.

Sometimes the struggle to go on is overwhelming. Victoria's room—and everything in it—remains exactly as it was. I sometimes sit on her bed and imagine that she is still here.

Victoria was independent, and she loved attention. She was smart beyond her years. She was always very artistic. I remember when she was only about a year and a half old, I put a pen in her hand. Before she could even write, she could draw perfect circles. She also loved to paint.

Victoria was a very good big sister to her three

younger brothers and three younger sisters. She loved taking care of people, and she also loved taking care of animals, especially her favorite rescue dog, Zen. She volunteered often at a local animal shelter. She was a free-spirited, happy, hippie pre-teen.

But that all changed—slowly and almost imperceptibly. When Victoria was around 15 years old, she started to have anxiety. She didn't like our family being a part of the movie *The Queen of Versailles*. Plus, she was being bullied in school, especially by the girls.

I took Victoria to see a psychiatrist, and he prescribed Xanax. Little did we know at the time that this was the event that would seal her fate.

Victoria became more and more withdrawn. She stopped spending as much time with us. She struggled in school and with her friends.

She was able to graduate from high school, but right after that, she moved into a guest house outside of our home. In hindsight, you might wonder how I couldn't have known how addicted she was. But I didn't. All of the warning signs were there, but I just didn't see them. Teens can be masters of deception.

Victoria's dad, David Siegel, and I only became

> I just fell into a deep sleep dreaming sweet dreams and knowing how much you love me and I'll always be with you. Take my journal in my nightstand drawer. The fat one I always use. I've never shown anyone my journal but there's no one else I would rather pass it onto than you. My business is everyone else's business now and I'm ok with that mom ♥ hey maybe you can publish my teenage journal and bump up your career. If it worked out I'd b so proud of u. I'll always be proud of you And I'll be right beside you when u win your first Grammy award. U won't be able to see me, but I'm sure you'll feel my peaceful presence holding your hand on stage. Now don't freak out I'm only trying to let you know I'm there for u. Always have been, always will be.

aware of the full extent of her drug use when we read about it in her diary, which she had kept hidden in her room. After Victoria died, her ex-boyfriend Matt forwarded the text at left to us that she wanted us to read if she was no longer here.

When I learned about Victoria's diary, I felt an overwhelming sadness. I found her diary right where the text described: in her nightstand drawer to the left of her bed. I carefully took the diary

out of the drawer. My heart was pounding. With shaking hands, I held Victoria's diary, and I read it.

And it broke my heart.

I couldn't believe how much Victoria had suffered. Her life was dark. She felt she was never good enough. After reading Victoria's diary, I felt like I knew my daughter better than I had when she was alive.

With a very heavy heart, I went to the living room, where David was reading, and I told him about the diary. He said he couldn't bear to read it.

Victoria had said in her text that she hoped her diary could be published to help other people who are struggling with addiction. She would have wanted to help them—to make them know that they aren't alone and to encourage them to get help. To get well. To be happy.

The heartbreak we have gone through losing Victoria is immeasurable. David and I don't want a single other family to go through this pain. That's why we have decided to honor Victoria's wishes and publish her diary. We feel that this is a way for Victoria to reach out after her death. Her words won't die; they will live forever.

As a mother, I wouldn't have ever wanted to expose Victoria's personal, most intimate, deepest thoughts. But because of her text, I'm following her wishes. It took me more than three years to be able to share her intimate thoughts with the rest of the world.

David also wanted me to carry out Victoria's final wishes so that her words will live on. Now I'm ready to share her legacy to save lives.

This book shares the story of how a beautiful, smart, funny girl with everything to live for—and despite her family's help, love, and support—became dependent on drugs.

This book details a story about teenage life—its celebrations and craziness, dreams and nightmares, hopes and addictions.

I hope this book serves as an eye-opener to parents that their teens could be experiencing these dark thoughts right under their noses—which is what happened to us. I also hope this book shows teens that they are not alone in their thoughts.

Introduction
by David Siegel

Victoria was full of life. She was bubbly and athletic. She was a natural leader.

One thing I especially admired about Victoria was her ability to always see the good in people. She saw the best in everyone, and she always tried to help people become even better.

Victoria also loved animals, even from a very early age. She volunteered at an animal rescue. She took all the time she needed to nurse a hurt or sick animal back to health.

Victoria always chose to help the animal that no one else wanted. She'd say, "Dad, I might be his last chance." We still have her favorite dog, Zen. He's the ugliest dog in the world. Yet Victoria saw the beauty in him.

As Victoria got older, she became more of a free spirit. She was quite a hippie! Even though our family had all of the money we could have ever needed, she preferred to wear comfy clothes

and walk around barefoot. One of Victoria's dreams was to open a sushi restaurant on the beach with a sand floor. She vowed to prohibit shoes, and she planned to put cubbies inside the door for people to store their footwear.

I always called her Victoria, but her friends called her Rikki. She wanted to call her restaurant the Rikki Tikki Tavern.

When Victoria was a little girl, she liked school, but by the time she got to high school, she dreaded it. She started skipping school. Her grades were poor. I worried that she might not graduate, and I think she graduated just to prove me wrong.

Victoria was quite the social butterfly. She had lots of friends, but as she got older, the girls got meaner. She also worried a lot about her weight. I think these combined pressures got to be too much for her sensitive spirit. I think that's why Victoria turned to drugs.

I wish I had known when Victoria was 18, before she died, what I know now about drugs, the epidemic, and the tragic consequences of teens' drug experimentation.

America is under attack, not only by terrorists, but also from the inside, due to the drug epidemic.

In 2016, 66,000 people were reported to have died from drug overdose. That number increased to approximately 72,000 in 2017 and by another 30 percent in 2018. More than 200 people die each day. It's like a jetliner with 200 passengers crashing every day, and we don't even hear a whimper.

We are losing our future generations. We could be losing the cure for cancer, inventions we will never experience, movies we will never see, books we will never read, music we will never hear. We could be losing our future Bill Gates and Steve Jobs.

As horrible as this sounds, there is light at the end of the tunnel. The epidemic can be ended, but it's going to take tough love and determination.

People are dying due to ignorance. A drug called naloxone was invented 47 years ago and is FDA approved and 100 percent safe. But almost nobody knows about it. If a person is lying on the ground, turning blue, and one breath away from death, a naloxone or Narcan spray in the nose will have them sitting up and talking within two to five minutes. This buys them 90 minutes, which is enough time to get them to an emergency room for treatment. Drugs such as opioids coat the receptors in the brain that control breathing. Naloxone cleans off those receptors, and breathing begins again. It's like turning on a light switch. Yet most of the people who need naloxone the most—drug addicts and their families and friends—have never heard about it.

I believe that a major contributing factor to the drug epidemic is the fact that many states are approving medical marijuana, which is a stepping-stone to recreational marijuana. People are voting to approve medical marijuana, thinking they are helping people who suffer from conditions such as epilepsy and stage IV cancer. The sad truth is that there aren't enough people who truly need medical marijuana to make an industry. The marijuana dealers are counting on your children using it for their profits.

Almost no heroin addict begins with heroin. Most addicts start experimenting with marijuana around age 14. Then they graduate to heroin, prescription drugs, or both. Marijuana is the gateway drug.

Sadly, we don't even need to legalize medical marijuana. A drug called Charlotte's Web, which is made from marijuana but has very low THC—the component that makes a person high—could treat people who need medical marijuana. But that's not well known either.

I believe that the only way to keep your children off the drug path to destruction is to start drug testing them at age 14. The fear of getting caught is the greatest deterrent against starting to experiment with marijuana. If a child has already started using drugs, the threat of testing is the best way to get them to stop. Testing is also the greatest defense against peer pressure. When a teen's friends say, "Be cool and smoke a joint with me," he or she can say, "I'm as cool as you are, but I'm afraid I'll get caught." If drug testing reveals that your child is using drugs, he or she will need counseling and possibly rehab.

I fear that until we get schools to start drug testing their students, we will never end the epidemic. Most private schools do drug testing and can claim to be drug-free. Sadly, few public schools test, and teens can buy any drugs in their hallways at any time.

I believe another major contributing factor to the drug epidemic is that most rehabs have 30-day programs, at a cost of around $1,000 a day. Most insurance companies pay only for 30 days. The problem is that it takes more than 90 days to cure an addiction. During 30 days, an addict can be detoxed and counseled—but not cured. To make matters worse, at the end of 30 days, addicts are at their most vulnerable. When they come out of rehab, they often fall off the wagon. They go back to the same dosage they were taking when they

went to rehab. However, their bodies are no longer accustomed to that high dosage, so they often overdose and die. The sad truth is that if you can't get your insurance company to pay for at least a 90-day program, you are better off not starting the process.

When my daughter Victoria died, I decided to dedicate the rest of my life to fighting the drug epidemic. I traveled the country and spoke to as many experts on the drug epidemic as I could. I met with the Surgeon General and the head of the Drug Enforcement Administration. I visited numerous rehab facilities. I spoke to Congress and helped push the CARA act, the largest drug bill ever, through Congress. I've spoken to numerous organizations—tens of thousands of people so far—about the drug epidemic.  (For more information on our work, please see "Our Advocacy" on page 287.)

Today, I consider myself an expert in the field. I used to think that drug addicts lived under bridges and slept on park benches. How wrong I was. Drug addicts are found in every level of society. In fact, the more affluent parents are, the more likely their children are involved in drugs.

Victoria's legacy is that because of her death, many more people will live. That's my promise to her. I'll work the rest of my life keeping it.

Victoria's Story
by Jackie Siegel

When I was 31 years old, I was living in Miami, Florida, producing the Mrs. Florida pageant. My pregnancy with Victoria was a surprise. When Victoria's biological dad found out I was pregnant, he split. I was scared.

Fortunately, I had a very healthy and happy pregnancy. I was happy to be starting a new life. The ultrasound tech had a sense of

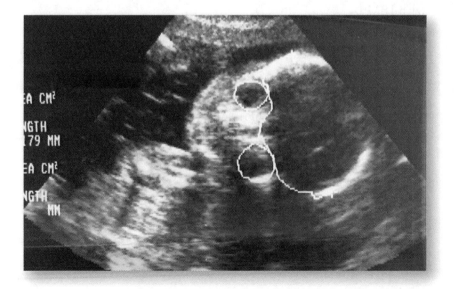

humor, and he drew some glasses on Victoria in the ultrasound photo on page 23.

Victoria was born on November 25, 1996. I felt excited, yet nervous, to be a new mom. When I left the hospital with Victoria, I remember thinking, *They're going to let me take her home?* Victoria and I began our life together.

Victoria was not a happy baby. She had colic, and she cried all of the time. Sometimes she cried so hard that she turned purple. Fortunately, she grew into a very happy toddler. She was quick to smile, quick to laugh.

I came from a big family that was happy but poor. I studied computer engineering at the Rochester Institute of Technology. After graduation, I worked three jobs to make ends meet, including waitressing at Red Lobster. My first job after graduation was with IBM.

In 1990, I quit my computer job and moved to New York City to pursue my modeling career. I enjoyed a fun single life, including dating Donald Trump for a bit. I met him when I was a model on the Trump float during the Columbus Day parade.

In 1997, at a friend's birthday party in Orlando, Florida, I met David Siegel. He was in the process of building his business, Westgate Resorts. He was newly divorced and really depressed at the time. I was head over heels!

David proposed to me during the IllumiNations show at Epcot on New Year's Eve in 1999; it featured their largest fireworks display ever. We were married in 2000 at Westgate Resorts Orlando. Victoria was a flower girl. She was the hardest-working flower girl ever. She threw rose petals all over the place up and down the aisle.

David adopted Victoria when she was just one year old. He brought her right into his heart, loving her as much as any dad could love a daughter.

Victoria wasn't an only child for long. Our son David was born in 1999, Daniel was born in 2000, and Debbie in 2001. After that along came Drew in 2003, then twins Jacqueline and Jordan in 2006. We adopted my niece, Jonquil, in 2007, after her mother—my brother's girlfriend—died of a drug overdose.

Victoria embraced her big sister role. David and Drew followed her around like puppies. Victoria and Debbie shared clothing. Drew and the twins all looked up to her. She loved to play with them and help them.

As an elementary schooler, Victoria was independent, funny, and smart. She seemed to love school. She especially loved art class, drawing, and painting.

I had always enjoyed competing in pageants, and Victoria followed in my footsteps. In 2004, when she was seven years old, she won the Junior Miss Intercontinental pageant.

Victoria enjoyed taking lessons such as dance, and she also

participated in a lot of activities, including cheerleading. As you can see in these early photos, she was a happy kid!

I always thought Victoria was beautiful, fit, perfect. But as she got older, she started to perceive herself as chubby. The girls especially started to tease her about her weight and also about our financial success. It was brutal, and it severely damaged Victoria's self-esteem.

I believe this is when Victoria's sadness with the world began.

In 2008, David's mom, Victoria's grandmother, died. This was a very sad time for Victoria.

When Victoria went to middle school, she became more and more preoccupied with her weight. I was concerned. I observed a cycle of eating/starving/eating. When Victoria was 12 years old, we sent her to a weight-loss camp. I had hoped it would help her self-esteem. It didn't.

I think the bullying at school kept getting worse and worse. Victoria tried to make friends by giving gifts and money. But that made her wonder if the kids were truly her friends at all.

At home, we enjoyed doing things together, especially painting and swimming. We moved to our current, beautiful home near

Orlando, Florida, in 2006. We had many cherished traditions, such as getting our family photo taken at the holidays. Victoria especially enjoyed it when our whole family was together.

We were fortunate that David's business with West-gate Resorts flourished. We were able to take many happy family vacations together. We especially enjoyed going to Utah, Daytona Beach, and Gatlinburg, Tennessee. Our children all enjoyed skiing and mountain biking.

One thing I noticed early about Victoria that continued

her entire life was her empathy for other people—and also for animals. Victoria talked about becoming a vet someday. She loved to rescue animals. She had a soft spot for the injured, sick, and ugly ones! One time she adopted a Chihuahua who was so sick he had no hair. Victoria found out he was scheduled to be euthanized the next day, so she brought him home. She saved his life.

Victoria's favorite pet was a dog that she rescued. I remember once she went on a school trip, saw a dog, and begged to bring him home. When Victoria was young, our home was filled with pets. At one point, we had eight dogs, seven cats, white peacocks, and even white tigers in our menagerie! I had to send the tigers to a sanctuary when they got too big and started acting dangerous!

In 2008, while I was shopping at a store in Los Angeles, I met a film director. Little did I know how that chance meeting would change our lives.

The director offered me the opportunity to star in a movie about how David and I were building the biggest house in America. The film crew practically moved in with us 24/7 for two years. For me, it was an enjoyable process. I didn't realize how damaging it was for Victoria.

During the filming, Victoria felt she had no privacy. She also felt that the movie had presented our family in a bad light. Then when the show aired, the kids were horrible to her. Victoria had tried hard for her peers not to know how wealthy we were. But now suddenly they all did. I later learned she felt it was the worst time of her life.

David and I tried to encourage Victoria's health and happiness. In 2009, when she was 14 years old, she did a photo shoot. She really seemed to enjoy it.

In 2011, Victoria went to high school. She hated it. She often tried to skip school. I was so worried about her mental health that I took her to see a psychiatrist, who prescribed Xanax. It didn't seem to help.

Victoria's friends were increasingly bad kids. When they came to our home, they stole things—money, laptops, anything they could get their hands on. I feared that Victoria might not graduate. But she did.

After graduation, Victoria moved from our home to a separate guesthouse. She had wanted to move out, and I thought this was a good compromise: She'd have some independence, but I could still keep an eye on her. This turned out to be a fatal mistake because I had less control over what she was doing and where she was going.

I began to be more aware of Victoria's drinking and drug use. One day in 2015, Victoria thought that she had taken too much Xanax. She didn't think she was going to wake up, and she typed a "goodbye text." She sent it to her ex-boyfriend Matt.

Fortunately, she did make it, and the next day she came to me.

"Mom, I need help," Victoria said. She asked me to take her to rehab.

I took her. And that's where she met the "love of her life."

He turned out to be a 26-year-old heroin addict. Meeting him set in motion a tragic chain of events that led to Victoria's death. Our lives would never be the same.

Publisher's note: The pages that follow are scans of Victoria's diary. Some pages have been omitted, and names of Victoria's peers have been obscured for privacy. Victoria's handwriting varies significantly, becoming harder and harder to read the more affected she was by drugs and alcohol.

In some entries, Victoria addresses her friend Korina. The two girls sometimes passed their diaries back and forth.

The following page is the cover from Victoria's actual diary. Her diary begins in early 2012, when she was 16 years old. Victoria had just changed to a new school. She writes about her close friendships and dutifully logs homework assignments. Soon she begins to talk about drug use and obsessing about her weight. Friendships suffer. Physical problems manifest, and her emotional challenges worsen. As the diary goes on, Victoria vacillates from happy, healthy teen ("what are we going to be for Halloween?") to troubled teen ("what's the point when there ain't nothing to it?").

This is Victoria's Voice.

My Teenage Life in a book :)

This journal belongs to:

Rikki Siegel ♥

Parts
my
of photo
shoot x
♡

Things that have made
me who I am
today.

And I live with
no regrets.

Project X # 2
Invite-Only Event · By

Going   Invite Friends

When   Today at 8:30pm

Where

Get Directions

Details   Its about time for a good ass rager!
We r pretty loaded up but bring
whatever you can to
at around 8:30pm.
DJ/ALC/TRIPPY/RAGE parking for
14 cars on the lot then gates get
locked so cops cant fucks with shit.
call me

EARLY 2012

"MASTERFUL. A WICKEDLY FUNNY ALLEGORY ABOUT THE AMERICAN DREAM."

THE QUEEN OF
VERSAILLES

JACKIE SIEGEL

www.JACKIESIEGEL.NET
www.THEQUEENOFVERSAILLES.NET

most embarassing
thing of my life. I'm
just happy her
dreams finally came
true.

I'll love you forever
mama

hey thereee! its my first day of school at crenshaw & its so weird! everything seems so messy & out of order. i dont even have my schedule. where the heck am i supposed to go!? so my english class was ok, except that my teacher said if we dont talk for the whole class period, we get a 0. The principal scares me, she honestly seems like a crazy lady who goes on a rampage when things dont go her way. Theres a few people who go here that i already know, ▮▮▮▮▮ ▮▮▮▮▮ ▮▮▮▮, ▮▮▮▮▮ and ▮▮▮▮ ▮▮▮▮. But grants not here today. Kimber was supposed to go here but shes moving to connecticut.. Whaso i decided to be friends with alex again since im gunna be facing him every day at school now, i cant stay mad @ him forever! he invited me over today but i said no because i have a hair appointme @ 3 & i have to go get new glasses since my whole bag got lost somewhere at our lake eve party. well the page is almost up o thats my que to go, Deuces!

-RILEY;

August 17, 2012

So its my second day of school and so far this school seems like a complete mess, but im not complaining. Its just that i have no idea where im supposed to go and neither do any of the teachers because they dont know where to place me! I dont even have a schedule, but quite frankly, I dont mind not having any classes(: I have to go to Olympia after school today to get my report card so mrs crenshaw knows where to place me. I'm trying to make this like my school diary so that means I have to write a page a day! Theres a lot of computer work here but sadly I didnt bring my computer today so I have nothing to do. im so hungry but for some reason i havent really been eating. I got my hair done yesterday and NO ONE NOTICED! or maybe just no one cares lol. The classes today seem much different then they did yesterday its so weird. I dont even know which class it which but this doesnt even feel like school. It feels like a camp and its still summer. But i guess thats a good thing! Im just happy its Friday already lol PARTy @ HOUSE! Baiii 💋 - R...

Some people say they don't get drugs, But I live in the moment and love them while they last because our past, future forever just nothing lasts as our ones becomes

live in trippy. Just Peace, happiness & Trust NO MAN, LOVE

Fear no

Belive in yourself + Think happy Be happy

Bitch

Crazy mutha fucka, i am one but the crazy this is, I began one.

This is my life!!! osoho

Rikki Siegel

RIKKI SIEGEL

RIKKI Siegel

Rikki Siegel

RIKKI SIEGEL

rikki siegel

BEAUTY is in the eye of THE beholder

2012

September 24 ♥

To the moon

These people, oh gosh. I hate them at times but love always overcomes the power of hate. I introduced them a while ago and they fell in love. And theres absolutely nothing I would do to to change that. I love these guys so much even after all the shit they've put me through. They've put me through so much that I can basically fit through any thing now. I will never for these two peso even when the earth burns to ashes.

and back 🌙

homework

+ write a 5 paragraph report on invasive pond species. Ecology.
+ Finish president worksheet, watch debate on T
+ Study for science succession test Friday.
+ sell 30 boxes of cookies.
+ study for vocab test
      (oak tree - hard wood)

homework

- study for ecology test Friday.
- sell 30 boxes of cookies.
Know what manifest destiny is, expansion, Result
on mexi-Ameri war.
- study for American history test.
- ecology word search.

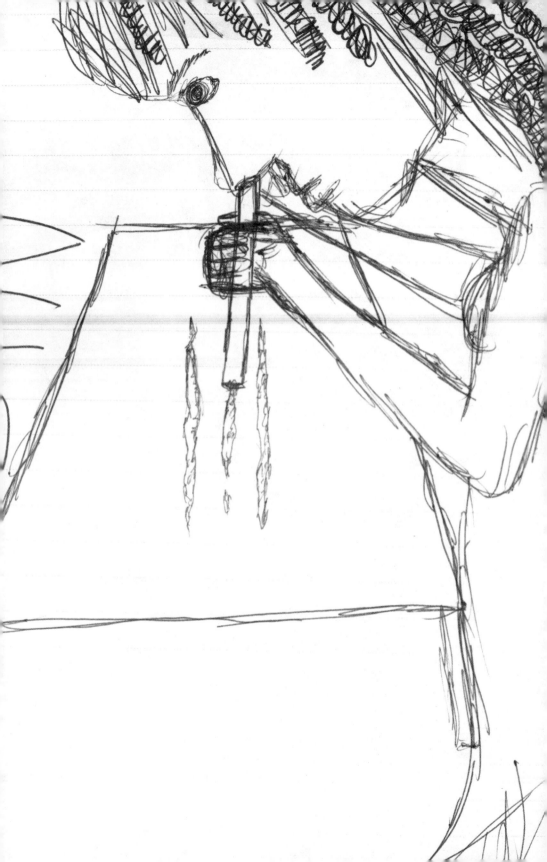

Finally came off!

I'm a bit of a clutz...

gross

I Ripped my toenail off by kicking it into the back of someones shoe running from security #Addrenaline #smoking #joints #in #hallways. (LATE November 2012)

I tend to loose elements belonging 2 my body often.

~~There~~ so many ~~things~~ stupid things I'm gunna miss doing.

What I think of love.   December 15, 2012

love, its a word. somehow made up in
the human mind. You can't put a label
on a feeling that strong. Some people
have been "in love" multiple times.
So how could you have possibly "loved"
someone you walked away from? I believe
that love means never having to say
you're sorry for hurting that person. But
I also believe that the expectations of
love go too above and beyond for a
species of our kind. Animals, in the
wild, mate with anything. They
dont feel love. Love is nothing but a
figment of our immagination. Its
an over-exaggeration of 2 people
being overly infatuated with each other.
For that period of time, to be exact.
Nothing lasts forever. Animals may
feel joy, companionship, partnership. But
love, it was created by people. Its
all in our mind. If we believe it exists,
we search out in hope of finding it. But
often get dissapointed. I guess in all actual
I think love is in this world somewhere, but
people's expectations of what it really is,
make it difficult to find. The only thing
I can say i have, and will love forever is family
friends may come & go, but family is forever.
                              -Ria Liz Siegel

I've lost all my friends.
how? good question...
I don't know, things are just
different now. I started going to
a new school and ever since then,
no one bothers with me anymore.
Its like everyone's just forgotten
about me. Comes to show who
your true friends are when you've
got nothin left to offer but your
friendship, Or I guess when
the going gets tough, your
friends get going. Lol. I probably
have about 3 people I can call
my "friends!" one of them is my
dog, and the other 2 are people
who probably won't stick around
for much longer. Like everyone
else, people come and go. I guess
that's why I have no feelings.
Because everyone is just plain
cold hearted as fuck. In the
end, Its just every man for
themselves. Getting drunk alone
on a Monday night because Im
a depressed fuck who doesnt
wanna study for midterms
tomorrow. But anyways, I'm
more than just a rebound. I
won't always be here when you
want me. Fuck friends.   18 of decemb.
       -Ria L.17 12:00 am

November/December 2012'
Some of my pictures from a photo
shoot w/ Elite modeling in California
i'm ugly, so i'm picky
w/ my pictures

December 22
2012

First Club I've ever been to
and it was fuckin' awesome.
didnt even have our Fake ID's
cuz we just that G~! lol or just
good luck shitters.

CLUb

Merry Christmas!
I'm tired so im not writing much
but this Christmas was pretty
chaotic. Too many fucking fights.
but on the bright side, i got supa cute clothes,
earrings (which i can't wear lol), a really
cute tiny camera, weed, & a Mac computer!

Finally.

OMG. so Jeremy, Frodo, & Leah
crashed the golf cart today and broke it
not like similar occasions like that
havent happened before, but i'm so over it!
because now i'm grounded and i wasn't
even there -- whatevaaa.

I was kinda in the middle of cleaning
my room but got distracted. oops. okay
well happy Holidays!

and i say that in the most
Buddhist way i can haha.

12/25/12
Btw: We didn't die 12/21/12 so hahaha
to all the bitches who believed in that shit.

I've come such a long way!

~~Before~~

2 years ago: 198 pounds. (12 yrs. old)

2 weeks ago: 149 pounds. (16 yrs. old)

Now 12/26/12: 125 pounds. (16 yrs old)

Beaty is pain and ~~pain~~ eating just is'nt painful enough. But i'm good at faxing it (: But shhh, thats our secret! no one can find out I dont eat. I'm scared to get put in some mental hospital :(

But who gives a lovely mutha fuck ass ▓▓▓. as long as i'm skinny. But its funny... I see my ribs, people tell me i'm getting too skinny, but yet I still think i'm obese. Is that a phycological problem?

YORO! guess im phsyco lol.

Dancin' up on stage in club w/ ♡
this crazy bitch

If you love somebody, you obviously had your reasons,
and those reasons will forever stay.

But i still will never trust her
or be close to her lol.

POT

Weed! Now legal in
Colorado (I think it
was Colorado)
Wahoo! one step
closer to Florida.

2013 PLEASE be the
year.

2013

2014: lol, still never happened

This New Years wasn't so bad ♥ even though i didn't go out and party on the most important day of the year, its a new year and thats all i could ask for.

I spent my new years packing till 4am for Utah. Which i think was AWESOME by the way. I was so worried it would suck because i had no bars, no adderall, no weed, NOTHING. But seeing as i always find my ways (i i had my resources!

- And of course there was alcohol!
So yeah, best family vaca ever ♥

The Big Year.

The craziness of 2012, things I'm able to cross off my bucket list.

- ✓ Smoked a J in a hotel hallway
- ✓ snuck into club ~~████~~ w/ no ID at all
- ✓ Scream "Fuck the police!" to a police officer
- ✓ throw the craziest party ever in a hotel room and NOT get busted.
- ✓ don't eat for 2 weeks
- ✓ sneak the car out ~~████~~
- ✓ get skinny
- ✓ find Narnia in the woods.
- ✓ dine & dash! (or try)
- ✓ loose my virginity
- ✓ get my permit
- ✓ do drugs
- ✓ never say no to any drug offered
- ✓ learn to be more brave.
- ✓ get too fucked up to remember
- ✓ steal a cute pipe
- ✓ throw a party every day/night for a week straight.
- ✓ Shrooms @ universal
- ✓ get in a fist fight
- ✓ stop worrying about myself/
- ✓ get good at rolling blunts
- ✓ run away
- ✓ smoke in a church
- ✓ escape cops! oinkers.
- ✓ car hop / steal a car
- ✓ ~~████████~~ Kiss a girl
- ✓ sneak parafaneilia through the airport
- ✓ smoke on a cruise ship.

- ✓ smoke in school
- ✓ convert to buddhism
- ✓ get legally banned from somewhere (M&M)
- ✓ go to a rave on molly
- ✓ throw up from raging too hard.
- ✓ go to school on acid
- ✓ go to school drunk
- ✓ trip on shrooms @ a party
- ✓ break someones heart
- ✓ get an adderal prescript
- ✓ get a rolex
- ✓ find myself.
- ✓ get a Fake ID
- ✓ steal something expensive.

Lets see what this year holds, ya?

hi, I just
found these and tho~~u~~
~~this~~ I should share.
mmm.... Pirates.
January 7, 2013 ———
New year, New level of weirdness!

January 7, 2013

Cisero's
Ristorante & Nightclub
306 Main Street
Park City
435-649-5044

MARYLANDMATCH.COM 800-423-0013
PRODUCT OF INDIA

Man oh man I love this place and i love snow boarding.

I did my first jump this trip! yay.

lol guess who checked in a week before we came? Justin Bieber!

OH MY GOSH!
i know right? Watch out guize I got a bad case of Bieber fever and its contagious.

lol who am i kidding? hes like 12.

January 16, 2013

I Finally went to the dr.

he said I was diagnosed with anorexia nervosa.

I think he's going to try to get me "help"

#1.) ~~xxxxxxxxxx~~ I don't need help!

#2.) I'm not anorexic

&

#3.) how the hell am I "too skinny" when I'm still fucking fat!?

OMG

Bitch i'm the bomb like

COKE!

i'd put a little of the actual thing in here but I always end up taking it in my times of needs.

TICK, TICK

My grandma drew me randomly @ a restoraunt.
I love her so much. lol probably becouse shes a
sagittarius too. She'll always hold a special place
in my heart.

My mom gave me this chocolate.

It smelled good,
felt good,
and looked good.
I just don't know how it tasted.

~~good~~ I almost had to
taste it. I was so close.

but I couldnt do it. I'm just
not ready.

So I'm saving the wrapper ~~from~~ for it so
that possibly I can taste it someday.
When I'm ready.

❤   I shall wait till then ✳

me ♡

the talent i had
before i knew
it (:

The truth about me is,

im not just your average human.

nor am i your average girl.

What may appear on the outside,

is nothing compared to what lies beneath this costume.

If you can be my boat, I will be your ocean.

I will keep you afloat when your anchor drags you down

I'll be the scale that balances you out when your lopsided

i'll be the road sign that guides you in which direction to

I will be the one to push you over the edge when your too

afraid to jump. But i will also be the one to

catch you when you get near the bottom.

I'll be the last one holding your hand when everyone

decided to let go. I'll hold your pinky with mine

and swear to never let you fall.

Because if you fall, I'd be the one to take that fall with you

When you look in the mirror, i'm what appears to be on

the other side.

Because when it comes down to it,

The truth about US is that we are all the same.

For we all have good intentions,

but our differences come from our bad decisions.

For I am the circle that never ends,

and thats how long I'll be your friend.

Judging a person does not define who they are,

it defines who you are. I'll be the one to read

you like a book but also the one to listen to

you read me one.
Some may say im a dreamer, a philosopher even.
But maybe one day we'll find the place where our
dreams and reality collide.
I live in the moments and love them while
they last, Because nothing lasts forever as
our future becomes our past.
For I am a sagittarius.
I am a philosopher.
I live in a dream world hoping that I'll never wake up.
i am a dreamer, But im not the only one.
And thats the truth about me.

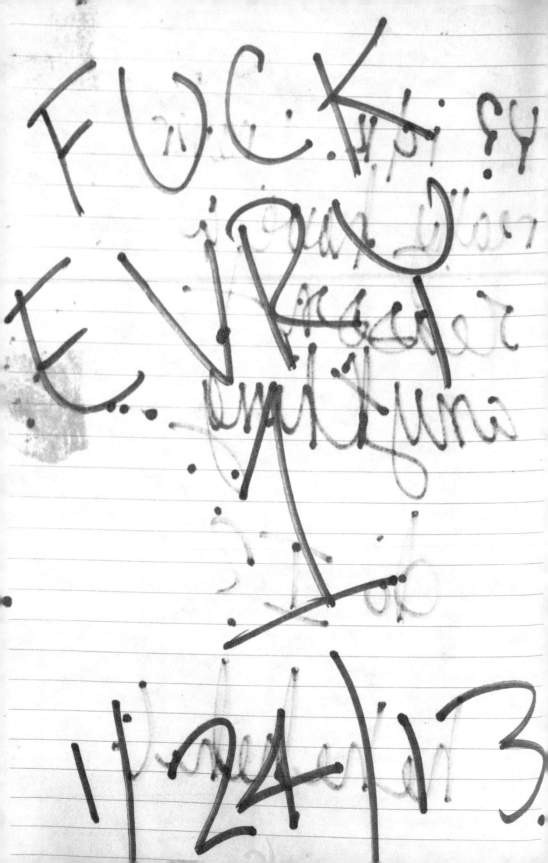

LOL! got caught crushin ofc at work 2013. FUCK!

from lab results - found when I first found out the hypothyroidism. :(

Patient Inf

SIEGEL.

DOB: 11/
Gender:
Phone:
Patient ID

407 029 4901

Dear Carlos —
Please take care
of Victoria —
She has hyperthyr
newly diagnosed
Sie

Test N
COMPRE
PANE
GLUC

UREA NITROGEN (BUN)	
CREATININE	0.80

Patient is <18 years old. Unable to c

BUN/CREATININE RATIO	8
SODIUM	142
POTASSIUM	3.8
CHLORIDE	104
CARBON DIOXIDE	25
CALCIUM	9.4
PROTEIN, TOTAL	7.5
ALBUMIN	5.0
GLOBULIN	2.5
PLATELET COUNT	
ABSOLUTE NEUTROPHILS	5359
ABSOLUTE LYMPHOCYTES	2478
ABSOLUTE MONOCYTES	487
ABSOLUTE EOSINOPHILS	34
ABSOLUTE BASOPHILS	42

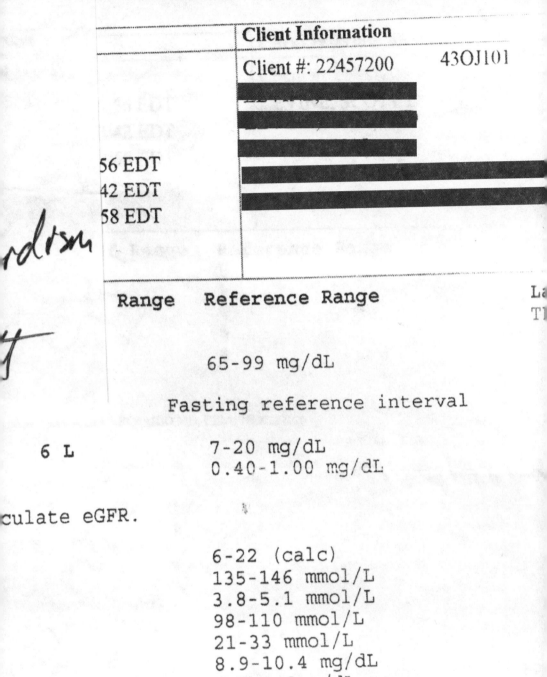

56 EDT
42 EDT
58 EDT

rdrsm

Range   Reference Range   La
                                    Tl

65-99 mg/dL

Fasting reference interval

6 L   7-20 mg/dL
           0.40-1.00 mg/dL

culate eGFR.

6-22 (calc)
135-146 mmol/L
3.8-5.1 mmol/L
98-110 mmol/L
21-33 mmol/L
8.9-10.4 mg/dL
6.3-8.2 g/dL
3.6-5.1 g/dL
2.0-3.8 g/dL (calc)
1800-8000 cells/uL
1200-5200 cells/uL
200-900 cells/uL
15-500 cells/uL
0-200 cells/uL

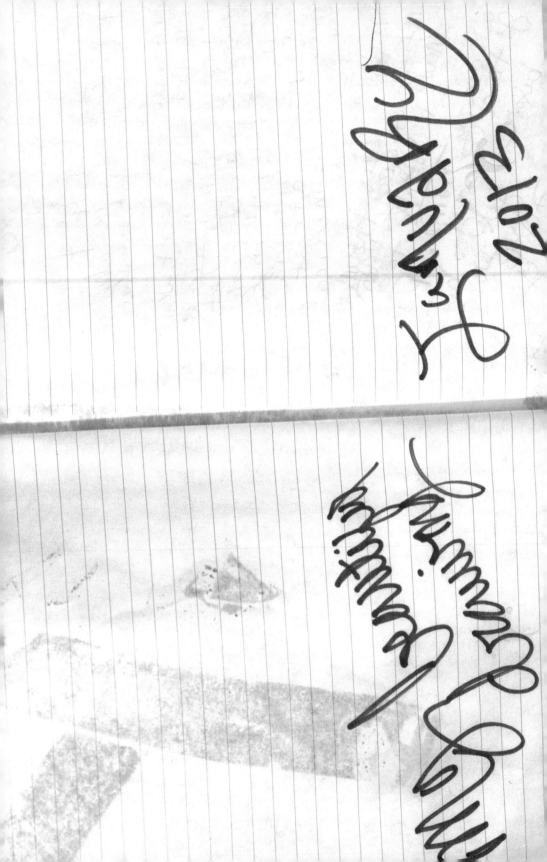

I am the beauty of the green earth and the white moon among the

Stars

wanna escape reality so lets a somewhere unreal.

don't explain your thoughts... there's no one really there to listen.

I've caught this disease called life to find the only cure is death

2013
February 18   Monday

I just snorted coke & I
feel great. but I'm
not really quite sure why I
decided to throw that out there.

I'm annarexic & I don't want
to go back! for once in my
life, I feel skinny. Thats
all ive ever wanted. if only I
could get everyone off my ass
about it. I don't wanna
see a psychiatrist
anymore. His medications
made me go mad.

I've never legit thought
of myself as crazy until to
now. I WANT to go to
a crazy home. I NEE
to go to a crazy home
before I get worse.
SAVE yourself

Homework

- Study for Vocab test Monday.
- Finish cumulative review
- ~~Finish cumulative review~~
- Fill out Vocab. 1-4
- Read act ~~xxxx~~ & write a ~~3~~ 1 page
- test for Othello on Monday
- Tuesday big Vocab test.

EM

krippady

ALL THE VOICES IN MY HEAD

through all the sleepless nights

when I've gone mad.

They dont
leave me alone.

every man 4 themsel

people care about

Mom   grandpa
dad   Kayla
david   Leah
daniel   Fadia
Debbie
drew
Jacqueline
Jordan
Karina
Hannah
McKenzie
Brandon Yeoman
Grandma
Matt
Mo
Raina
Emily
Paul

FUCK LIFE

what's the point when there aint nothin to it?
People die.... but people also move on. time heals everythin

Live in the moments love them

Live in the moments while they and love them while they last because nothing lasts forever as our future becomes our lasts past. forever a future b ou

Live in the moments and love them while they last because nothing lasts forever as our future becomes our past.

Live in the moments and love them while they last because nothing lasts forever as becomes our future lasts as our future our past.

and live in the moments and love them while they last because nothing lasts forever because as our future becomes our past.

Live in the moments and love them while they last because nothing lasts as our future

Rikki.
Before anything

Pills Pills

Some people say I

Pills Pills Pills Pills Pills Pills Pills Pills Pills Pills Pills Pills

laugh, giggle, smile in

Pills Pills Pills Pills Pills Pills Pills Pills Pills Pills Pills Pills

my sleep. Pills Pills Pills Pills Pills Pills Pills Pills Pills Pills Pills Pills Pills Pills

Well thats because im at the one place that makes me happy. Pills

@ Peace. Pills

2/4/13

sleep sleep Pills Pills Pills Pills Pills Pills Pills sleep sleep sleep sleep sleep sleep sleep sleep sleep sleep

Hi. Its time I thought i'd do a free write of what I can't really come to my senses about. I will be straightforward and hold nothing back. 2013, I stopped eating, doing more drugs to make that process easier for me. Not eating led to an eating disorder "anorexia nervosa." This problem later led to a severe depression. I came to my senses & realized it was time I get help. I developed insomnia aswell. My mom brought me to a psychiatrist he didnt care about the anorexia. He was more concerned about my depression. He prescribed me depression medication, which kinda seemed to be working at the time. Then there was the Lorazepam for anxiety & to help me sleep, which I obviously abused because its similar to Xanax. Then there was my insomnia medication. I wasnt complaining about anything. I thought I was being fixed. little did I know things would only get worse. My insomnia had gone from just not being able to fall asleep, to not being able to stay as then to just not sleeping at all.

→

I realized what was keeping me awake this whole time. My mind. Something else was controlling it that i couldn't escape. I began seeing thing that didn't make sense, that werent really there, I began to hearing things So loud, so clear, so real, they would shock me from my slumber. I lost my mind, i thought. Gray hair began growing from my head & disgusting blemishes plunging from the surface of my skin. So much stress, I went insane. I told every one of my experiences, then i realized that rather than listening, they were still establishing just how crazy i really was. But no matter what anybody says, I was with the devil that night. I felt him, saw him, heard him. I know what happened & it was something I'll never be able to explain. So I saw my psycho'ologist again. Told him of my experiences @ night, explained that I still wasnt getting any sleep. At school, i was getting hallucinations from lack of sleep. Eyes playing tricks on me. He then decided to keep me on my dep- ession pills, But gave me another epression medication to take w/ it.

he also gave me two different super
strong sleep medications to be sure I
see to my sleep. & last but not lea[s]
he gave me a medication for
schitzophrenia to take every night.
I KNEW he thought I was crazy
too. But I saw the one flaw w[/]
what he was doing. How could a
body that doesn't eat & get the
nutrients it needs to survive, han[d]
all the medications being put into it
w/o having a hard come-back?
   It couldn't. I took my medications
that night, tried getting a glass of
water before they kicked in, but wh[o]
knew it was only a matter of secon[ds]
my body grew weaker & weaker.
by the minute until I was crawling
to my moms room on the floor. I
was shaking so bad, & I was so
weak that I thought I might never
wake up again if I fell asleep. lol
But funny how I woke up around
3am & I went back up to my room
for the night. The stupid medicati[on]
didnt even work. That experience
scared me so bad, I decided [t]
throw all my medications away. Th[ey]
are what were making me crazy
crazy.

it had gotten to the point of not being able to be happy if I wasn't taking my depression medicine. But I realized, if I wanted to fix myself, I was going to have to do that on my own without the help of these monster creating pills. I'm not gunna lie, it really sucks. I can't remember the last shower where I wasn't crying hysterically w/o reason. I'm so sad, and so alone, all the time. I don't like it, but I WILL escape this feeling on my own.

It has to get worse before it gets better.

3:00pm
2/18/13

ya?

Till   I still retain
    there   this   hope
Rikki

my mom says this was a Xanax withdrawal.

Historical photos I
found of this one
happy family

So crenchaw decided they're
gunna start drug testing me
LOFUCKINGL!

I told em i was gunna
show up positive
ofcourse, like who the hell
do they think i am!?

haha, OT
watch watch out,

Rixxi Fuckin Siegel
is comin'
back ♡

BTW, Raina is going to move
in w/ me whenshes TB, which
will be this year during
November. 11/22 i think
gosh, if i'm right i am SUCH
a good friend. E

shhhh....
2/20/18

OH BTW! I got charges pressed against me for "drugging" Rgina F & grant got charges pressed for "Raping" her. LMFAO! Ya I laughed Too.

But its all cleared up now. Turns out her dad made up everything because he's Fucking psycho.
I'm convinced.

Lololol.

So me & Raina are good now. She just cant see me till shes 18, Which I think is dumb.
But I guess all I can do is wait & hope for the best ♥

This is Rikki...
Calling out,
"chhh" hehe (:
2/20/13

one thing i've learned is that no friends are forever, only an entertainme for the time being. I do believe there are real friends out there, but they're difficult to find. Don't be fooled by a mask. ~~xxxxxxxx~~ NOT my friend. ~~xxxxxxxx~~ NOT my friend. ~~xxxxxxxx~~ NOT my friend They're only good for keeping up an image.. but once you stop caring about your image, They stop caring about you. But i'm okay with that, because it shows me everything i need to know about them. I do best on my own anyways. As long as i know that people will NEVER change.

So long Ko, or wait... I think the words you used were.....
later hoe li   lol

am I the only one in this town who knows how to grow up?

looks like it.

♥

-3/17/13

caffeine free
subtle tea.
cannabis activated chai tea
NET WT .07oz (1.9g)

the VENICE
COOKIE co.

Despera
times ca
for
desperat
measure

drank it @ school w/
urns out, it doesnt work too well unless u
drink the whole thing.
Now this is what I call
my cup of Joe

MCO   EZM
Mini Coin set

$6.99

5693

Why are these coins so
Effing cute!?

My madre buys the weirdest
shit lololol

- 3/19/13

Buddhism.

The four noble truths:

1. __Dukkha__: suffering exists
2. __Samudaya__: There is a cause for suffering. (it is the desire to have & control things.)
3. __Nirodha__: There is an end to suffering (the mind must let go of any desire or craving)
4. in order to end suffering, you must follow the eightfold path. __Magga__

The eightfold path:

Panna: Discernment, wisdom:
- Understanding of the four noble truths
- Right thinking; following the right path in life.
- Sila; Virtue, morality.
- Right speech: no lying, criticism, condemning, gossip, harsh language.
- Right conduct by following the five precepts.
- Right livelihood; Support yourself w/o harming others.
- Samadhi: concentration, meditation:
- Right effort: promote good thoughts; conquer evil thoughts
- Right mindfulness: Become aware of your body, mind, & feelings.
- Right concentration: meditate to achieve a higher state of consciousness.

The 5 precepts:
1. do not kill
2. do not steal
3. do not lie
4. do not misuse sex
5. do not consume alcohol or other drugs.

too bad i've kinda
broken all
except 1.

Reincarnation!

which isin't
been part of
~~Bud~~ Buddhism
lol, its part of
that shit

forgot what its
called

— 3.19.13

oh... how thoughtful.
not everybody gets a letter
with their pants.

oh, & did
Acid for the 1
time w/.
Layla

My mom & I had a talk.
     she told me who my real dad
                              was.

FINAfuckingLY !!!
he's an Italian police officer who
 lives in Miami. he left my mom
when he found out she was pregnant
w/ me. P.O.S.

She & my Aunt Jessie say I look
  just like him.

 his name is ████████████.
I just wanna see a picture of him.
       thats all...

I also found out that Siegel is
 a jewish name. &
█████████████████████████
█████████████████████████
█████

The strange thing is that I always
knew David wasnt my Real
dad. I guess it was just an instinct.
& I've always had a fascination
 w/ everything Italian. I guess
its just always been in my
     blood.   3/20/13
     xoxo   - Rikki Mangan.

I was totally devastated
when I found out.. but I
finally told my mom &
she actually made me
feel alot better. I
realized, never place a
period where life has placed
a comma. everythings going
to be okay. That was one
hell of a crazy week
though. Jumped from my
balcony twice on shrooms, Daryn
basically moved in in w/ me
that whole week. Took out my
mom's bentley to take trittty
to school, got caught, & can't
remember driving home, & now
I'm back @ olympia. Holy shit ma,

1 overheard my dad talking
2 some 1 on the phone
about sending me to
a rehabilitation center
in ft. Lauderdale.

Sounds like fun pops.

but he thinks i'm getting
better, but I think i'm
just too convincing &
so he doesn't notice i'm
worse than ever.

but kinda do wanna go
to that rehab.. Xanax &
Adderall widthdrawals
really scare me.

BTW, I got ▓▓▓▓▓▓
high today !! she was
SO cute ♡♡♡

April 27, 2013 ♡

last night i had a dream of my paradise. A place so amazing, so beautiful, so new & exciting, nothing i could say would be able to explain it.

Water so blue, sky so clear, temperature perfect, mountain Islands so forest green you couldnt stop exploring each & every one of them & their qualities. Creatures so mythical & so scary @ times, but you were never injured by them & their mythically abnormal qualities were so normal to the location they were in. You were always doing something. though there were creepy people, there were also hot, cool people. I would give ANYTHING to go back, even if it meant falling asleep forever just to live there...

April 27, 2013

OH! i 4got 2
mention that i
got prescribed
Klonapin.
(Clonazepan)

mind I say,
i'm kinda diggin'
it! I'm just dying
to get it refilled.

And also, my phone got
stolen @ a party my
senses warned me not
to goto, but ofcourse i had
to make hannah & Ko happy.
iphone 4, here I come
A/27

I know I'm wrighting a lot,
but I'm only trying to
catch me up to date...
If I make any sense lol.

I don't even know what to
call this book, is it a diary
or what?......

Theeee.... book of random?
um... how boutt.... oh wait
im dumb...
     its obviously already
got a name lol.
     my teenage book of life.

    oh fuck it,
  guess what date it is!?
       you'll never guess...
muahahaha.... ok, huh?
how'didya know?
         oh poopie.
whe. 4/27... why am i such a
                    dork!?

4/29/13

how did i fall so far behind? to the point where i legit have to RELY on my depression medication? I hate it. Something makes me hate everything. I'm suprised i havent written anything about this yet.. but ive been cutting myself. The ONE thing i thought i would never do. But the pain makes me not have to think about all the other hurt in my life. I have no idea whats been going on in my mind. But the worst part is not being able to remember how i felt before. When happiness was an element of my mind that i believed would never run out. I've also gained a lot of weight, I can see it in my face... i'm going to stop eating again, I just don't know what else to do when everything turns to shit. -Rikki ess

btw, just a reminder!
- Period ended 4/28

Not to mention, I've stopped
going to boxing, mainly because
my knee has been killing
me & doest necessarily
want to get better. & ever
since Crenshaw didn't want
me, I've been fucking everything up for school.
What else will happen
to make my depression
even worse? LOL! if thats
even possible because I've
already attempted to kill
myself multiple times.
My attempts just always
fucking fail. but thats
obviously nothing new..

E-mergencie's only essy!

BTW, I CHANGED MY ^MIDDLE NAME 2 ESSY.
I'll SHOW YA HOW!

VICTORIA → VICKY & RIA → RIKKI

ELIZABETH → E Z E → ESE → ESSY

YA I KNOW IM QUITE THE ODD ONE.

WHICH IS EXACTLY WHY EVERYONES
JUST GOTTA LOVE ME!

-RIKKI ESSY ♥

THE QUEEN OF VERSAILLES
ORIGINAL STRAW...
THIS WILL BE WORTH
MILLIONS SOMEDAY!
BUAHAHAHAHAAAA

<u>JK</u>

LUH YOU DOE MAMA ♡

MY BABY PIGGLY THE PEANUT.
A 200$ STUFFED ANIMAL ONE
OF A KIND THAT MY DARLING OF
A MOTHER PRESENTED ME WITH.

I THINK I LOVE
IT A TAD BIT MORE
THAN A NORMAL PERSON
SHOULD LOVE THEIR STUFFD
ANIMAL.

OK FINE I LIED..
A FUCKTON MORE

HAPPY TIMES

THE TRIP 2 UTAH THAT I BELIEVE
HONESTLY CHANGED MY LIFE.

MAN OH MAN MY HOROSCOPE
WAS SO RIGHT ABOUT GREAT
LOVE IN THE MONTH OF MARCH.
OR ~~GREAT~~ GREAT SEX I SUPPOSE.

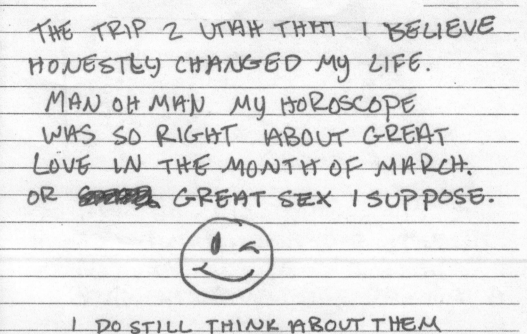

I DO STILL THINK ABOUT THEM
SOMETIMES THOUGH. I JUST TRY TO
ABANDON THE THOUGHT SO I CAN
HOLD MY HEART TOGETHER IN
ONE PIECE. BECAUSE I KNOW
THAT IF I PUT MY HEART IN SOME
ONE ELSES HANDS, THERES ALWAYS
THAT SLIGHT SLIVER OF A CHANCE
THAT THEY'LL SQUEEZE IT TOO HARD.
AND A HEART CAN ONLY HEAL SO MANY
TIMES. YA FEEL?

WHICH IS WHY I'M THE SMARTEST
COOKIE IN THE JAR. ITS JUST SUCH A
SHAME THAT I'M THE ONE WHO GETS
EATEN RATHER THAN BEING THE ONE
WHO STEALS THE COOKIE FROM THE JAR.

if im wondering why all
my $ is gone, its probably
b/c i took it all out to buy
drugs & alcohol. I'm dumb.
So get this... I got
tresspassed from westgate.
I have the paper &
everything w/ my thumb
print & shit. what are
the odds? what am i
gunna do when we go to
Utah? where am i gunna
get my hair done!? &
who the FUCK is gunna
find the coke in the hotel
room air vent? hahaha.
My pops thinks me & Ko
we're running some mad
prostitution shit w/ a 21
year old b/c of the fake
ID the room was under.
& my dads the one who called

the cops to have him
arrested... I always
knew there was something
I hated about that man.

He wouldn't even let me
come home for a couple
of days so I've been staying
w/ Ko. I'm going home
½ day the 8/10 my mom
gets back from France.

Soo something's wrong w/
my memory, I forget a lot
of shit when I drink as
if I were on bars. That
never happens. & I get
majorly stupid. like I walked
into Ko's moms room late at
night thinking it was Zander's.
& Ko's mom caught me taking
a pair of Zander's swim shorts
b/c I said I wanted to "sleep
in them." like wtf. that makes
no sense to me b/c Ko's room
was right next to me & I could
have easily borrowed something
of hers. Her mom asked me what
I was on lol. I make myself
look so domb in front of her. — June 2⅞

What i want for X-mas! 2013

- Combat boots
- my glasses
- Keyboard
- Polaroid camera
- Clothes
- #
- a car
- Professional camera
- Candles
- Rolex
- Punching bag
- Dance classes
- Boxing lessons
- Sound system for making Dubstep
- TOMS
- Running shoes
- Trip to England/anywhere

actual hand →

why do I do that? why am I like that?
how do I manage to fuck up every-
good thing I have going for me? Am I
afraid of getting too close with someone? is it a deep dark past that
haunts me? Do I cause pain to
myself to escape/prevent other
pain? is it my provacative mom?
over protective asshole for a Dad?
what hole am I trying to fill by
pushing away everyone I love?
why do I allow myself to be used?
why am I okay with people using
me? is it because I know that the
people who dont truly care about me,
cant care enough to be hurt by me? i
dont know whats wrong with me. But maybe
I'm just a stupid fucking cunt. I want to
get in touch with reality, But I view
things too differently to relate so
easily. I'm sad, & by that, I mean I'm
a sad excuse for a friend. If I were
talking about feelings, broken, would be
the word I'd use. I don't like what I
do. So why do it? good question. I need to
grow up. But I feel like I've grown up
too fast, I feel like I've hit the peak
of my life & my world is coming to an
end. I hurt you, but I hurt myself
worse. i'll never be able to forgive
myself. literally. I try to hold back from

crying so hard everytime I think about you & realize your not mine anymore. Its so terrible because half the times I cant. Theres not a day that I wake up w/o thinking about now I defied you, not a night where I fall asleep hoping that I wont wake up unless I wake up next to you, i can't eat, I can hardly get through the night i can't talk to anyone, I cant even ACT like i'm happy w/o remembering why I have to pretend in the first place. I was doing so well in school when I had you by my side, in my life, Now, I dont see the point in getting up for it anymore b/c I dont have you to come home to @ the end of the day anymore. I didnt go to school yesterday, I tried not to go today I havent done one single assignment, & I just cant ever seem to be on time anymore. I dont see why, I dont bother getting ready in the mornings, i cant even care about hygiene anymore. So what If I let myself go? I don't see a point in caring fors for my health. I havent changed in 2 days. My new method of getting ready for school in the mornings is crying to myself so that I wont be seen crying in school. I try to act like I dont care, but I do.

I think I care too much sometimes, so I try not to care @ all. It doesn't work out so well for me but nothing ever does, does it? Anyways, I don't know what the point of this pathetic passage was. I know you gave up on our books, I guess I'm just ranting because I have no one else to talk to & its always nice to pretend your still here, b/c I will never give up on you.

If you end up reading this, I love you, I love you so much it hurts. so much that I don't know what to do w/ the love your afraid to accept from me. I go crazy. I want to come be with you every second of everyday but I fear you'll kick me out, I fear you wont take me back, & I especially fear that things will never be the same. I could right forever b/c I just feel like this is the closest I'll get to speaking w/ you. besides texting ofcourse, but I just can't seem to be as sincere

through a text as I can on paper. I
kinda have the same issue speaking
to people in person. I think I'm
just so overwhelmed with what is
happening @ the moment that it
literally takes me a good while
before I can actually grasp the
concept of how the situation will
affect my life. It's like, when I'm
apologizing in person, I give off this
"I don't care what I do" type of
vibe, But believe me I do, I care
so much. But only if it affects someone
I care about. like you.

You will always be my
closest family & will always
hold a place in my heart.

I love you so much that all the
love I have for you has to be
jammed into my heart, taking
up the space meant to contain the
love & care I should feel for others.
But there are no others, there is no
one else I care this much about,
no one else I care to have ~~you~~
in my life. no one ~~else~~ else worth
the fight, which only leaves me
with a heartache. Sometimes you
have to sink to rock bottom, you can
before

find the right direction to swim up
for air. I don't know if I've hit rock
bottom yet in my life, but I know
I've hit it in our friendship. & I
can't hold my breath any longer. I
know which direction to swim in now
if I ever wanna breath again.

Till death do we part. which is why
you can't leave me yet. b/c I need you.

　　　　－Wikki.

9/27

life.

feathers of life.

I love you.

life is like a
feather. I don't
know why... it
just is. deal.

10/1/13

Hello AND A HAPPY Tuesday!

I just took a test & had to name all the bones. I sooo aced that shit. Pshhh, eazy peazy. I miss you. I kinda wish we weren't such lazy bums & we had went to hhn that night w/ my family. I think it would have made my mom happy. But enough of that nonsense! When are we getting our tats? I ~~w~~ can't wait much longer o.o

O - M - fucking - G! guess who gets their 'sence in 29 days? US

I'm super psyched. I hope I get my car back — love you. Rikki

Korina. C.

THE XANAX DOCTRINE

So I know were getting bars today & I also know why I shouldn't be doing them. But since I know, I, <u>Victoria Elizabeth Siegel</u>, vow to consume these xanax in a slow moderation, So slow that we will have some left for halloween, I promise I will take no more than two in a time period & I will <u>NOT</u> take them if we will be seeing Brent. Though, I know I would be able to control myself, I want to stay clear from all possibilities of fucking anything up. I promise to be sure I know exactly what i'm doing when i'm doing them. I will take them only for special occasions & learn to save them rather than take them @ any time simply b/c they are there. I will maintain my self control and go to all extremes to make sure we have a kick-ass time doing so.

Sincerely,

But whatever happens...
we MUST save them for
halloween. But I'll also
wanna shroom the fuck out
on halloween. That'd be
pretty raw. So I'm waiting
on Daryn to come get me
from panera & I fear we
might hook up. IDK what
it is that makes me so
attracted to him. OMG
awkward, hes here, gotta
go, I love you mucho gusto

     -Rikki

         ↑

  ew, NOT anymore

I wasn't talking
about the "I love
you" part btw. The 10/10/13
hot anymore was
directed towards Darryn. But I guess thats
kind of a dead give away lol.

favorite pic bk it looks
like me,

❤️ mommy

haha, I love how i previously said we MUST save the bars for halloween but we have none left & halloween is still a month away. As you can tell, since I was obviously barred out/ barred over in the previous few notes. This weekend was crazy, I finally got to punch Alex, Brent got away, you got stabbed (Real ████ shit), & @ the end of the day, we still went out & got FUUUCKED up. You even went to the hospital & got 12 stitches that night lol. I cant believe it happened outside of moes... that was dumb & we probably shouldnt have dealt w/ straker @ that location. But YOLO! People driving down sand lake probably thought someone died b/c of all the cop cars/ambulances/ helicopters. Which somebody would have if you didnt take one for the team & get in the way of Brent killing Alex right there in the parking lot. Could you imagine having a murder investigation on our hands? Our ~~goooopotooold~~ family would be in Pretty little liars instead of skins 101. Well, no. That was a terrible example, but ya feel

this kid next to me likes writing you notes too... So he going to write u one now.

P.S. We have to go get tatted soon since the shop was closed that day.

P.S.S. We better get our laptop back from Tevin b/c we both know we finna kill a bitch if we dont.

I love you
bye.

his name is Ajay now →

These few weeks have been great. I actually feel like im in a family. its me, Korina, Brent, Peachy, chris, nick, & I guess sarah. Notice how I didnt say Alex? well thats because hes a fuckbitch who stole my brother's laptop, BOTH their IPHONES, & Peac. script of yellow ladders. oh & lets not forget my Ipad that I was trying to sell. Everyone blamed Brent (Peachy's Best friend) & Peachy Beat the shit outta him. Kinda like how im gonna beat the shit out of alex when I see him. Who the fuck is stupid enough to take Picture of all the shit you stole oh yea. ▓▓▓▓ FUCKING ▓▓▓▓ FUCK FUCK. ▓▓▓▓▓▓▓ ▓▓▓▓ dont you have something better to do? like go get your dick circumsized fuck bitch. lol thats kinda the new word around here. Everyone keeps calling sarah that to fuck w/ her but I dont really mind her. its just that she can sometimes be an annoying...... whats the word i'm looking for? oh yea, FuckBitch! BtW, everyone is off to get me & Korina a script for Barz under sarah's name

iok how theyre doing it but I don't
give a lovely mother fuak ass
     I'd forget the reason
anyways takin all them barzz
speaking of Korina, we both got
matching tattoos of a lotus
flower on our ribcage, everyone
loves it. We're gunna be best friend
4 ever & I just know it. I love her
more than I've ever loved any
one in the world. We're going to
Utah tomorrow & I cant
fucking wait.

I ♥ my
Family

Chris

me   ko   Sim   Brent   peach   Rick

I'll stop for a few days
& then run it all w

eating something.
I'm @ ___ lbs.
I'm so fa+ it sucks.

but ya, you missed
my sticking straver.
terina got stabbed in

I have NOT been
keeping up w this
journal lately.
hmmm... what
have you missed?

OK. I gained a lot of
weight & for some
reason, I can't seem
to stop eating to take
the weight back off.
I'll stop for a few days
& then ruin it all by
eating something.
I'm @ like 155 lbs.
I'm so fat, it sucks.
but yo, you missed
me sticking straxer.
korina got stabbed lol.

its not funny but just lol.
We STILL went out
that night. We rolled
FACE. or @ least as
face as we could w/
the "molly" Peachy
had haha. Brent got
arrested last night &
is currently there,
me & Darren almost
had a thing but I
realized he doesnt know
how to treat me right,
I fucked Korina over
w/ Brent & I gave up
bars because I will
NEVER hurt Korina
like that again. But I
will still take them if
Korina is ok w/ it.
10/15

Korina,   9/9/13

hi, i miss you. i wish you'd come to
Olympia already so school doesnt
suck so bad. i'm in advanced algebra
for finance or some shit. David Ramsy
says if i follow his steps, i'll retire a
billionaire lol, this class is odd. Btw,
i think your drawing is pretty fuckin
dope. no wait, i don't like that word..
i think your drawing is.... Rad.
there we go. Our plans for when i get
my license.
- Summer road trips! ❀
  ○ first, i want to drive through
    Nevada, Las Vegas. stay in Vegas
    for about 4 days, go to Utah for
    like a week & ½. Then check out
    Colorado & visit   lol.
    we can stay there for like 2 nights.
    then we head back. i think that
    sounds like fun.
  • Then we need to take a roadtrip to Cali.
    we'll stay there for like 3 weeks &
    stop @ places on the way there &
    back.
  • & then one to NY!!
  • get jobs
  • save up for appartment.
This is gunna be fun!!
    love you - Rikki

9/10/13

I hate writing on this page. lol so I was thinking about our families. & I think this family was the best...

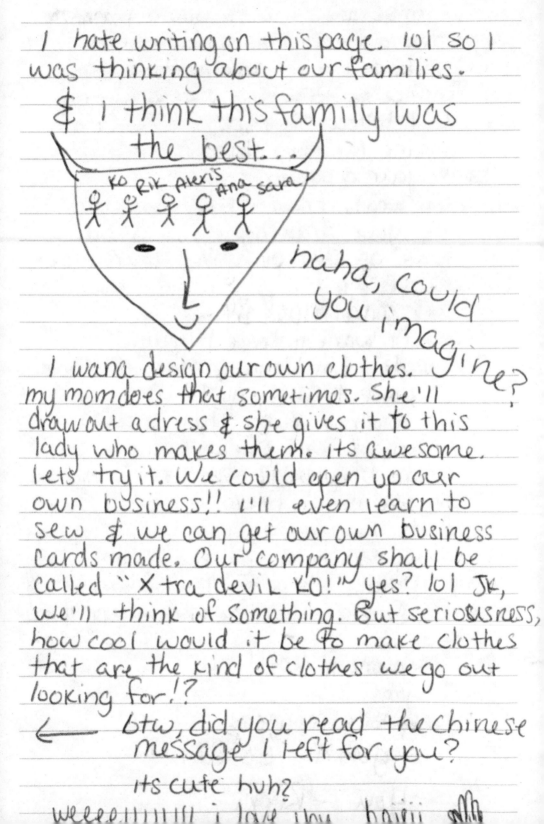

ko Rik Alexis Ana Sara

haha, could you imagine?

I wana design our own clothes. my mom does that sometimes. She'll draw out a dress & she gives it to this lady who makes them. its awesome. lets try it. We could open up our own business!! I'll even learn to sew & we can get our own business cards made. Our company shall be called "Xtra deviL KO!" yes? lol JK, we'll think of something. But seriousness, how cool would it be to make clothes that are the kind of clothes we go out looking for!?

← btw, did you read the chinese message I left for you?

its cute huh?

weeellllllllll i love you haiii 🖐

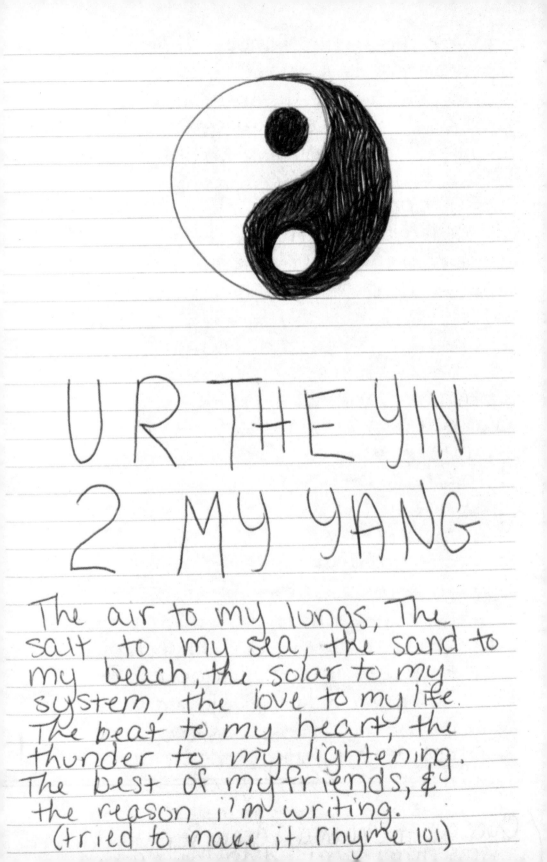

UR THE YIN
2 MY YANG

The air to my lungs, The
salt to my sea, the sand to
my beach, the solar to my
system, the love to my life.
The beat to my heart, the
thunder to my lightening.
The best of my friends, &
the reason i'm writing.
   (tried to make it rhyme 101)

Hi O˅_O I'm Lakyia (LmL)

I Fucking hate Ms. Scero
She's on that #Team #Fuck the
#Seniors. How are ya. O-O

Who are ya? Can ya read this?
my handwritting is terrible.
So since I Dk ya. I imagined
ya as a ginger. >-> With
emo hair and a black girl
voice. LoL ^_^

Fuck School. Fuck Sked.
   Drinking is Bad.
   Pot is good.

Yo mama so fat!! When
She walked by my T.v.
   I missed 3 episodes.

10/11

i'm getting better @ drawing this!

haha, do you think that if I asked for a tattoo gun for christmas, my parrents would buy me one? b/c I woul so love to try it myself.

i know what I wanna do w/ my hair! i've always died it blonde but never electric blonde or w/e its called. Its like that bleach blonde that is a little close to white. You know what i'm talking about? I'll make the appointments today after school. ARE WE GOING TO THE game today? Raygan I wanted us to go but she's been bothering me lately. Also, Tomorrow is home-coming so theres gunna be mad parties! baii <3 -Rikki

What we need to get for our minion costumes:
- Minion beanie
- yellow knee high tube socks
- goggles
- yellow bandeau
- white sneakers
- black gloves
- overalls/or high waisted shorts w/ suspender

* And I was thinking about carrying around like a banana or a small bull-horn so I can walk around & say "bee-dow bee-dow bee dow!"

(not sure if you remember that from the previews of Despicable me 2 when the minion is trying to sound like a police car or w/e)

♥ though the banana might be easier because we don't have to buy it & we can eat it if we get hungry lol.

P.s. skip school wednesday so we can shop till we drop.

if your a bird, im a bird.

10/17/13

hey boo, so as you can see,
im trying to practice my
cursive because it fucking
fuking sucks. I dont even
know how to do a fucking "k".
— by the time my b-day
comes around, i'll have my
license, so i've been thinking
about how were gunna
celebrate and I planned our
first road trip. we are
going camping on the beach.
how dope does that sound?
I just want it to be like
us & the family. But first,
we need to find a beach
where its legal to camp on
@ night b/c I also wanted
to have a bonfire on the
beach as well so we can like
roast marshmallows & shit.
I just want to live on the
beach for like a weekend
w/ the family.

   — what do you think?

- I get my license in 15 day
- I got the old Red Navigator
- Ive gotten my shit together
- I cut my hair & died it
  bleach blonde. like
  almost white
- I still hate ████████

Im so scared I wont be getting my license tomorrow. I just have a feeling it wont work. I feel like crying & my phone is dead. It feels almost unreal that the day has finally come. Tomorrow (cross my fingers) I shall be a designated driver. lets just pray to Buddha that all goes as planned. Shit, I'll wait in the line over night if I fucking have to. Though I'm sure they'd kick me out during closing time lolol. Me & Darryn got into a huge argument & I just blocked him & deleted his # cause I realized a piece of shit like that doesnt deserve me in his life. & I dont have time to deal with low life trashy ass bithes. There are things in this world that I would never wish upon anyone b/c theyre specialized for him & only him. I want him to suffer. e-nuff los talk. I gotta go, love you

BYE!

P.S. I dont think we have a costume yet... lol.

So it sucks I didn't get my license yesterday. It also sucks that it's halloween & I STILL have no costume, did you ever get one yesterday? I can't wait to hear your ideas! ANOTHER thing that sucks is that I got one of those court letters too. We're such criminals. They can't drug test us when we go there, right? LOL, the place I went to take my driver's test yesterday was the same place the cops took me to interview me about the whole Blue tree thing. I guess my court hearing is now Nov. 6 @ 11 & my driver's test is same day @ 2:15. I got dis.

So since I DON'T have my license for halloween, I gave sheri a list. I'll write it down on the next page. Brent has to sneak in somehow though haha, I cant put him on the list. You excited to see your baby!? aww I'm so happy for you, we'll pick him up on the beat or something.

xoxo - love you! Rikki

u kno whats awesome? The fact that you got ▓▓▓▓▓ to drop the charges. u kno what else is awesome? The other fact that I got these awesome colorful pens to write notes w/. Now they won't be so plain & boring! Its gunna be so weird seeing ▓▓▓▓▓ out now if it ever happens b/c I'm so used to the feeling of always trying to kill him. lol I totally 4got about the ticket nicholai got for wreckless driving. I feel bad, he's gunna have to pay it haha. Also, sorry about your wallet but I have confidence we'll find it (: I'm making our hair appts. Today after school. Hopefully I don't have to hear them bitch about missing our appts. last week, I'm just gunna say I got sick.

I LOVE you

RU

STORY TIME

Once upon a time, in a faraway land was an underwater moon in which all the rave fish would use it as a disco ball when they went out to rave & rage. Then, one day, a rock on rocket spaceman went to the bottom of the sea to find out what all the commotion was about. When he spotted their moon, he brought it out of water and threw it up into the night sky giving all the people light. Everyone was happ Except the rave fish who were left with nothing b/c the disco ball was what made them rave. They couldnt rave anymore so they became depressed & lost their color. Now they are mindless creatures. Thats ho the moon got in th sky & whu fish no longer dance THE EN 11/6

did easter already pass? b/c I
have a great idea for an
easter party.

We have an easter egg hunt
but instead of $ or candy
in the eggs, they are filled
with drugs. & everything you
find, you take.

like, different eggs would have
different kinds of drugs. The
brighter colors will be
stimulants, the darker
colors will be downers, the
eggs w/ designs on them
will be hallucinogenics, &
the golden egg will have the
best kind of drug that
everyone wants.

ya? So what do you think!?
b/c I think this sounds
crazy, in a crazy awesome
way.

I get my license
2day. Wahoo!

← arm

around
my right
arm.

11/14/13

bigger wolf head
& maybe no
music notes.

Kokina_____   11/15

to start the day off, i love you
i love you i love you & goodmorning.
my handwritings really bad today
cause for some reason, my hands are
really shaky. We're going to
Adventure club tonight!! I'm so
excited. We better make sure sidney
will still take us, I'll text her about
it now.... or right after I finish this
note. I cant believe you might
actually be going to school w/ me soon.
you have no idea how excited i am.

We Out!   I cant wait to
             get our tattoos!! I'm
just ~~math~~ kinda worried that that
place will mess it up. I'm just
putting all my faith in █████ lmao.
I'm in math & financial aid &
I don't think I've done 1 single
assignment in this class. I literally
pay this girl Jamie to make sure all
my shit on edmodo.com gets taken
care of. I ~~████████~~ just had to give
her 10$ for doing 4 of my
assignments. ~~████████~~ keeping up
100% A in this class is makin me
a broke ass ████ lol. I have $ to
get Molly, so lets try to get it from peach
bf we go to Adventure club. I also can't
wait to get zarred the F**k out xx

Man

Siddhartha
Guatama.

بيكون في سلام، لا في القطع.

be at peace, not in pieces.

12/4

Chew my love
under your tongue
like its your
bubble gum. Your
blowin' bubbles till
the taste is gone.
Your comin' over for   the
night, just one night, one   night,
one niiight. Chew my love under your
tongue like its your bubble
gum. Just spit me out
if it becomes more
than fun, you're
comin' over for the
night, just one night,
one night, one niiight.

YOU MAKE CASUAL
MESSY. and all   materials
possess   you like
a   slave.

YOUR CUSTOM !
made. ♥   —RIKKI

Its everywhere.   12/4/13

hate   anger   spite

rage   lost   lies

ashamed   lust

cold   scared   misunderstood

bored   hopeless

lonely   defeat   greed

hopeless   bitterness   broken

judged   cruel   insecure

impatient   sadness

isolated   anxious   ignorant

desperation   arrogance   insane

grief   envy   frustration

irritated   death   unhappy

ruthless

love   impulsive   complication

confused   sad   mad

jealousy   secrets

egotistical

irresponsible   sorry   rejected

paranoid   pain

frightened   victimized

manipulated

discouraged   insecure   outsider

pity   unresponsive

miserable

agony   unforgiving

escape

self-destruct   resentment

disappointment

no where to be found.

cared for   happiness

forgiving

truth   calm   brave

love   joy   help

guidance   accept

faith   simplicity   honesty

relief   understanding

bliss

open-minded   giving   hope

safety   sanity   tranquility

success   peace

friends   perfection

contentment   support

secure   reassurance   humor

courage   open-hearted

united   selfless

capable   innocence

individuality   luck

loyalty   confidence   life

productive   prepared   appreciation

stability   popularity

security   hope

comfortable   satisfaction

warm   valued   inspiration

worthy   appreciated   freedom

protection   equality

compassionate   tolerance

understanding

strength

Breaks over & its kinda depressing me out man. I dont wanna be @ school. I wanna be @ home w/ u driving somewhere to eat, making a serve, going to a friend's house. I wanna be lazy & still be laying in bed in my PJ's thinking about what were gunna do tonight; making jokes about how much of a profit were gunna make from smoking all our bud & then i'd say "haha, were such good dealers" then we'd laugh a little more & you'd ask me if I wanted to smoke another bowl. we'd laugh again & get high. Then we'd go home & take all my clothes to Plato's closet to make $ to re-up. We'd be the typical dumb stoners wondering why we ran out of bud so fast as were smoking a blunt in the car on the way to re-up. lol sorry i'm literally day dreaming over here so I can block out every aspect of school. I really want to find a job, a real job. one w/ no competition, one i'm good @, & one were my heart doesnt skip a beat everytime I see or hear a cop. I want to be responsible & make my dad proud. i'm just hoping he wants me to get a job. He wants me to just focus on school right now which is probably a good idea but I gotta make $ somehow! lol speaking of cops, I left the house this morning @ 5:50am to go get coffee from starbucks. We had like one bowl of weed left so I packed it in the bong & brought it w/ me for the road. I didnt want it to spill so I put it in the cup holder. (after I finished the bowl). Then I see a cop right next to me going down ████ ████ I turned into where I usually turn to go to Starbucks & he followed me. I started sketching out so hard b/c I thought he might've seen my bong in the cup holder so I took it out & held it w/ my hand in between my legs & parked. Then he parked too, right by me!! I couldnt breathe b/c I was about to have a heart attack. I couldnt open the door or windows b/c then he'd see the smoke coming out of the car so I stayed put. Plus I had the whole drug bag w/ the scale & everything in the car too. He got out of the car, started walking towards my car, then right before my heart stopped, he kept walking past my car & went inside starbucks lmfao. I started cracking up b/c of how sketchy I ~~was~~ thought I was being. I wish my dad wasnt such a douche, He says my curfew on school nights is 10pm & I have to sleep @ home on school nights (which i'm sure we can scheme around) & then he expects me to be in by 12am on ~~school~~

weekends. I think I work too hard ~~to come~~ on school nights to only get an extra 2 hour break on weekends. Fuck that, suck my dick Dad. (not really, ew). I wish i didnt have night school on Mondays & Tuesdays. Just more shit to deal with. But i love you & I gotta get back to earth now so i can make good grades. 101. Roger that.

xoxo - Rikki.

Problems w/ my car:

- Blinkers dont stay
- ~~brights~~ headlights are too dim
- brights are too dim & 1 doesnt work
- ~~scanner~~ scanner is expired
- almost ~~~~ @ a mileage of 200,000
- keeps saying "check engine"
- need more $ on sunpass.

♡ "thats all for now folks" ♡

KORINA ♡ 12/13

Hiiiiii! I'm happy you slept over last night. For some reason, I can only get a lot of work done when you're over. Ur my motivation :-

12/17

Some call you amazing...

But I just call you Mine ♡

"I'll always be your helping hand, time after time"

I'll spend a
life time just
to shine. But like
the moon & sun, you
spend a life time shining.

All on your own,
but together we
will rule the planets.

FOREVER &
ALWAYS.

12/17

its
Lost.

Find it.

Sometimes I tell myself I don't believe in love.
I DO.
But the fear of never finding it keeps me from believing. ♥

Love
Love
Love.

what is it good for?

Absolutely
NOTHING.

12/5 - 12/6

Eet - Regina Spektor

🎵🎵

lol sorry that song was just stuck in
my head. But my phone died last
night & I can't find my charger
ANYWHERE! it's really aggravating
me. it should b in my backpack.
But anyways, I'll have to just find it
when i get home & text or call you.
i think i'm sleeping over tonight if u
want me to! But i have to be @
Saturday school by 9:00am tomorrow
morning. ugh. shoot me now. OTAY
I LOVE U! c u after skool!! ♥

12/6
            - Rikki
               XOXOO

I dont understand. is it to accept?
The possibility of changing isnt relevant anymore.
The world seems lonely when people stop caring
doesnt it?

Its because the world stops loving you when people do.
People dont come back, do they?
what happens then?

when did we get so sorry for ourselves?

-12/18

When you're happy, try to remember that feeling.

Because once it goes, you'll never get it back.

Then you're left with nothing, and there's nothing you can do.

SO you're making
me write sumthang.
Well I love you
xoxo. so I ready 4
spring } break,
my bday, summer,
you're my very
bestfriend ♡
everything b|c I'll have you
by my side ☺

mythical creatures

fairies

Acid

India

reincarnation.

Trippy

witchc.

skulls

TRIPPY

INDIANS

Egyptians

DMT

DMT

Constellations

MDMT

trippy patterns

dream catchers

peace

patterns

death

dreams

Pyramids

myths

mermaids

INDIANS

monsters

wolves

i've been thinking about our T-shirt designs & I think all we really need to do is come up w/ a theme that surrounds the scene of our generation. heres some themes i've been thinking of.

- horoscopes
- buddhism
- religion
- drugs
- shrooms
- quotes
- animals
- animals on drugs
- nature
- photographs
- indie
- hip
- all of the above

I found an awsome app that shows you how to make all these awesome creative ideas. All the way from mini caramel apples to decorating your shower with Eucalyptice (or however you spell it) But I'm gunna find something cool & we can totes make it. Like this girl made lipstick out of crayons & it looked so easy! We just need coconut oil. it looks amazing. & it gives you really cool tips. like.. after applying 1 layer of mascara, put baby powder on your eyelashes & THEN put on another layer for a longer, fuller look. Pretty cool right? The app is called trusper. IT IS FREE. download it now. NOW!

downloading...

45%

Also, JCC is having a winter festival this Sunday the 26th. Can we go!? it sounds so festive & cute! OK its settled. We outcheaa!

I'm gunna get my whole head braided. dare me?

XOXOXO

-Rikki ♥

lol it'll b cute

1/24/14

I heard that the new hookah bar
that opened up by Colo Burger doesnt
ID ANYONE. Can we please check it
out!? this weekend!
_____ wants to go there too. IDEK if you like
her or not but shes a sweetheart. If
you dont want her to come, I just
won't let her know we're going. Idc, I
just havent been to a hookah bar
since I was friends w/ _____
haha. I just want a chill, fun night
outside the house. We can get
wasted & go dance @ the hookah
bar & we can tell all our friends
to come! Then we can eat @ CB
if we get hungry since they're right
next to eachother. This should be
the new chill spot, like were ppl can
meet up & pre-game or some shit.
Like instead of going to the sanctuary.
I think thats a great idea!

                P.S. Lets trade books
                    this weekend.

x90   -Rikki!!

1/27/14

We haven't been trading books b/c it seems as if you've lost all interest in yours :(You better step up your game girl! Jump back on that horse; or Unicorn. We went to such a weird party on Saturday, Not even words can explain it lol. A cop was there the whole time & randomnly decides to kick everyone out?

MIND FUCK!

I Finally got my parking hanger for school. Soo thats a plus! haha guess who I saw transferring to OT today? Kimber! speaking of which, when you starting school here @ Olympia?

Well, I gotta go but may the force be w/ u. ♡

XOXO

Rikki

See The way I
drugs it, phychedelic
from reality, are not a trip,
IC They are a trip
reality.

1/27/14

I must being steady. lol.

too bad, i cant write in cursive

Fuck, it.

FUCK EVERY
THING,
ONE,
FEELING,
Thought,
VOICE.

we don't have a voice, our thoughts misgui
us, our feelings betroy us, + it's every one
+ everything around us that makes
it have to be that way.
              2/9/14

There once was a girl 🧒. & she was so
sad all the ~~H~~ time. 😞 But she
just couldn't figure out why 💡? her
whole life she spent teaching herself to grow up 👨‍👩‍👧‍👦. She blamed
everyone around her for making her
so sad & miserable. She treats her Mothr
terribly. She feels miserable about it
but she can't help it. For some reason,
her mother changes the person she is.
though the girl of course loved her
mother to death. She used to be that
weird fat kid in school that got bullied. she
was ashamed of who she was. Her
parrents tricked her into going to fat camp
when she became semi-okay looking.
& then eventually she became one of the
"cool kids" you know. the kids who do drugs,
dont go to school, don't even bother w/
hw. Well anyway, she became so consumed
in that life that it broke her, it broke who she
was. She stopped eating. for months before
anyone had noticed, how annorexic she
was getting. her father was always too busy
w/ work. & he's getting so old she didn't
even know if he could tell how much weigt
he had lost to be honest. $

. I mean, wh
did you expect she get all the pills?, wee
alcohol?, cocaine? It just all went wrong
when she realized she could simply
get skinny by just avoiding food.
Those were the happiest days of her life
though. for once in her life she felt
confident. Beautiful. life she didn't
have to fuck anything that moved just
to feel like she was worth something.
When ppl began to realize she had a
problem, They finally decided to pay some
attention to her. Too much attention. she
was forced to see a psychiatrist where
he put her on all this medication
that made her insane. The point in
her life where she met the devil & saw
him laying in her bed next to her
& still believes that to this day. She
took advantage of her skinny good look
& became a slut. though she always dreamed
of being w/ the perfect boyfriend one
day, she realized she couldn't do it. she
couldn't be w/ s/o. no matter how
hard she tried, she always pushed
them away once they began to catch
feelings. She felt that she was doing
them the favor of allowing them to
find someone who they deserve, someone
better, ANYONE other than her for
that matter. She thought she was a wast

to the world & everything in it. She began taking pills every morning, day, & night not because she even wanted to But b/cause they were there & she said fuck it. she got drunk every night rather than doing homework. Not b/c she wasn't a smart, intelligent girl, but b/c she didn't have the motivation, that she was ever going to pass school anyways. she didn't care what happened to her. She became to do things to herself. bad things. dangerous things. But who noticed? no one. Just like no one noticed she had become anorexic it was so obvious in her face, tiny bony fingers in big baggy clothing. nothing but skin & bone underneath. Her school noticed her problem shortly though. They expelled her b/c they thought it was for her own good when it was really the worst thing they ever could have done. Now I'm here. & dead end rotten failure. slowly dissintegrating & dying from the inside out. She'll never be the girl she once

I love too much, thats the problem.

4/17/14

Why am I so bored all the time?

Why do I treat the ppl I care about like shit?

Am I a bad person?

Why can't I explain why I do the things I do? to the ppl I love?

Why do ppl care about living their life to the fullest when they won't remember it anyway?

If energy can't be created nor destroyed, where does it go when we go?

Where does it come from?

Why am I not afraid of death?

Why won't anyone just hear my cries for help?

what if I dont survive?

then I'll find the answers

what
if I dont
survive?

then I'll find
the answers
I'm looking for.

Gods & Monsters ♫♫

In the land of
gods & monsters,
I was an angel
living in a garden of evil,
Screwed up, scared, doing anything that I needed, shining
like a fiery beacon. You got
that medicine I need, Fame,
liquor, love give it to me
slowly. Put your hands on my
waist do it softly; Me & god,
we don't get along so now I
sing; Nobody's gonna take my
soul away, I'm livin' like
Jim Morrison. Headed tow-
ards a fucked up holiday,
motel sprees sprees & I'm
singin'; fuck yea give it to
me! this is heaven what I
truly want, Its innocence lost,
innocence lost.

Me & Ko finally fought ~~the~~ & I don't mean like a hissy fit, I mean like fist to face type of thing. I don't remember exactly how it went down b/c we were both barred TF out!

but we're fine now ♡

That's how I know she's a true friend. After her giving me a bloody nose & me giving her a black eye, through thick & thin, she'll always be my sister.

5/12

healthiest foods to eat: 5/12

- Grapefruit: helps build bones; prevents chronic diseases, improves eyesight, & keeps mind sharp.
- blackbeans: lots of protein, no saturated fat
- Oats: fiber, helps you feel full throughout the day, healthy carbs that boosts metabolism & burns fat.
- blueberries: anti-aging, helps satisfy hunger.
- broccoli: Cancer prevention, Cooked or raw.
- brown rice: boosts metabolism, burns fat, full-fills hunger;
- Pears: fiber & fewer calories.
- *Wine: stops fat storage; drinking 1 glass can boost your calorie burn for 90 minutes.
- Kidney beans: protein & fiber, slimming carbs.
- Almonds: healthy fats that help u slim down.
- green tea: fills u up, antioxidants burn calories & fat; 5 cups a day helps u loose twice as much weight.
- Lentils: protein & fiber, healthy carb that boosts metabolism & burns fat.
- bananas: slightly green, medium sized will help cure hunger & boost metabolism.
- oranges: cures hunger
- Pine nuts: burns belly fat, stalls hunger;
- white beans: fat blasting, boost metabolism.
- low-fat milk: Calcium; protein helps u feel satisfied.
- Garbanzo beans: slimming
- Quinoa: hunger-fighting protein.

June 15, 2014   9:15

I'm not ~~terrible about~~ ~~mood~~ ~~(bayoos)~~ ~~emotions~~
sad, angry, jelouse, suspicious, depress
loved, happy, excited, joyful, frien
united, special, outgoing, thankful,
regretful, ashamed, brave...
beautiful, ugly, smart, stupid,
talkative, hungry, full, creative,
loveable, willing, judging

I'm <u>nothing</u>. ~~~~

just useless. I have no point.
    so why the fuck
        am I still here?

        on this earth
    thats slowly burning
        to ashes?

        just b/c I'm forced to live
here, doesn't mean I have any
    use to mother nature, I wish
I did., but I don't. I'm sorry

I want things to be the way they used to be; where I could resist food & ppl, actually noticed & gave a shit. they used too... but they all think I'm better now b/c I've gained all my weight back; but truth is, I'm more miserable than ever but no one seems to have the power to see through me. Starving myself was the best time of my life b/c for a little bit, it seemed like ppl cared. But then they stopped & just left me to die. Starvation is the most peaceful death. You just simply fall into a deep sleep while all your organs slowly shut down. I'd die in my sleep & everything would be better. I just want everyone to know that if I were to ever pass away it's no ones fault but my own. I love you all & you all are the only reasons I've made it this far. dont ever blame yourself. I love you & till death do we part. live your lives in peace & I promise I'll be having the time of my life up there, for you

Forever & ever

6/15/14

I hooked up w/ matt again.
I didnt mean to.....
it just happened.
    But he told me
he loved me..

    LOVE.....

        LO sucking L

No. one loves me.

its just bull shit.

Matt told me to get birth
control today. or the
morning after pill......
I'm freakin' out man.

whatevs...

Rorina says we
must be infertile
so I'll take her
word for it lmao.

Summers almost over.

WTF!

whatevs. peace

I'll figure this shit out
like a boss

ugliest.
this is the one
I'm _not_ wasting

lol. I know....

waste of a page.

Fuck the
Fuck
outta hea!

So I'm back from my 2 week trip to Spain. lemme just give you a little update of what happened before we left. Carry threw us a going away party & Guess who showed up.....

FUCK BITCH ███████ HER & KO got in a fight b/c KO started talkin' shit & LEAH tried to hit her. I held Leah back lol who TF does she think she's messing w?

NE wayz our trip was amazing. We didn't get ID'd once & got so turnt. We even found a hash club that we got membership cards to & we got weed brownies.... that I left in the hotel fridge lol. we stayed in the el palace hotel. But I wanna cuddle w/ Frank B4 he passes out so I'll finish telling my story laterz. (i love ya' 1♥!

BRB.... lol, I'm back. a day later hahha. oops. But I fucked him haha oops.. again.

BYE

Funta#tic 5 & Friends   Miami 2014

Miami, hisami, her ami, all our ami & you
ami. hehe. WEIRDOZ.

LOGO IDEAS. Lets get TATT

2014 halloween

I'm gunna draw my costume ideas on these wasted pages.

numbered from fave to least fave

- Shroom ① — gold cap
- mermaid ②
- minion ⑭
- hunter (like catness) ⑥
- Savage ⑦
- Voodoo doll ⑳ ⑮ ⑨
- infected (Zombie but hot) ⑧
- cheshire cat ⑩
- deer ③
- fox ⑪ / wolf
- "when life gives u lemons" ⑰
- avatar ⑱ ⑳
- hippie ⑲ ⑲
- buddha ⑳ ⑦
- medusa ⑫
- skeleton ⑤
- alien ④
- pot head (pot on head) ⑳ ㉑
- blurred pixelated nude minecraft ⓵
- army chick ⑬
- comic book make-up ⑯
- beer mug ⑱

2014
9-13

my dad today told me that I'm a freeloader
all I do is "take take take & give nothing in
return." he said I do nothing for the
family. & he told me my life is
meaningless. But hes 100% right, I need
to get my shit together. he said I dont
have to go to college if I get a job, but
I DO wanna go to college. he just
doesnt believe me. he thinks i'm only
saying that so I dont have to work.
He doesnt believe I'll go to college b/c
I hated high school.. but i still did it....
didnt I? & he didnt even believe in me
when I told him I was gunna graduate.
He told Me I have to go out & get a
job tomorrow. thats gunna be a tough it
I should prolly be more focused on that than
what I'm gunna be for halloween ——→
lmao. Fuck it. I need something to take
my mind off of what he said to me for
a little bit so I can try & hold it
together. My father doesnt believe that
college would do me any good. But
I don't get that. Isnt that supposed to
be every parents dream for their child to
actually WANT to go to college? IDK but
I'll figure something out. hes also mad b/c
he says I do nothing good for my mother just
b/c I don't wanna be in her TV show. he
just doest understand. I just hope I get the
chance to prove him wrong some day. I AM a

Gold-cap Shroom costume

I call it the "Shroom Stume" imao

LED glasses

OR

Black kangt pupil contacts

Beach hat made into mushroom, spray painted gold

golden bra/croptop

Short gold/brown skirt

goes w/

goes w/

goes w/

high waisted gold shorts

OR

OR

gold/brown socks

long golden-brown skirt

goes w/

goes w/

goes w/

golden brown fuzzy slippers (uggs maybe)

* w/ gold body paint *
& gold lipstick

IDEA FOR KO'S ALIEN COSTUME

Antennas ←

Black costume contacts

lots of dark black eye liner

Black or green lip-stick

w/ or w/o → fishnet tank top (Black)

alien pasties ←

rave wear panties ←

or crazy pigtails instead of antenna (or both)

thigh high/ knee boots (with ...
s...
co...
got...
rav...

← the wear

← (or moon boots

faded green body paint & face paint

Dear 10/19/2014...,
        I think I'm finally
starting to find myself. I'm very
different now than I was then.
Not sure if its good or bad, I guess
both. I think I'm just finally growing
up. Its not as exciting as I thought.
I thought it'd be fun, ya know? But
nope, I was wrong, totally & extremely
wrong. It's scary. I feel like I'm
being thrown from an air plane &
IDK if I'm wearing a parachute
or a backpack. Med & Korina are
finally moving out.. like I mean its
really happening. I think we start
moving our stuff in tomorrow. Its
so weird, that feeling, those memories.. the ones that you look back &
& you just can't believe its finally
over. I don't know what happens next.
But i'm scared to find out. I don't
know if I WANT to believe its all
over. growing up is hard when no one
tought you how to do it. It's like im
stuck in the midst of space just hoping
some day I'll reach earth's gravitati-
nal pull again & i'll be able to once
again stand on my feet. I'm so terrif
of responsibilities, of fucking up, going
no where respectable in life, failing ppl,
failing myself.. I'll drink to the future!

10/19/14

I found this old pic deep deep in Mama's closet. I'm not sure ⊗ who the man in the pic is... its POSSIBL That it's david Siegel; "step Dad". But IDK, I can't see that well plus plus plus Plus its an old picture. But when I look closer.. I almost see a resemblance. Its like I see the guy whom my aunt Jessi' described who's suppose' my real "Father" I don' give a shit if it is or no I Just wanna know the tr But regardless, My B. father w always be the one I called DAD. The one who raised me the one who made me who I am today. XOXO — Ryan DR

HE

from beyond the valleys hi
and low, I watch the people,
as they go. with a peaceful
expression upon their face,
As he guides the people
to a better place. their souls
float up into the light, and he
promised to return them
when the world is right. When
something brings our planet to
an end our world will restart
all over again. when adam
and eve get a 2nd chance,
they'll make the right choice
and sing and dance. so we can
live without a threat And there will
be nothing to regret. When
all this happens we shall thank
"he", the one who put us in
this peaceful place.

Victoria's Last Months
by Korina Cockrell, Victoria's best friend

I met Victoria when we were around 14 years old, at a high school party. We went to separate schools. That's why we passed our journals back and forth.

When we first met, Victoria was very bubbly, full of personality. She liked to dress up and do her makeup and hair. She wanted to be doing things and going out all of the time. We went to parties every weekend, hanging out with friends. We went out on her parents' boat, and we often had people over. We shopped—a lot.

As the years went by, Victoria started to go dark. She let her hair hang unstyled, and she stopped wearing makeup. She wore old pants and old T-shirts all of the time. She didn't try to take care of herself; she didn't seem to care about her appearance at all anymore.

When we were 14 years old, Victoria started smoking weed. Then she started taking Adderall and Xanax. Then using cocaine.

The fall after we graduated from high school, Victoria and I moved into an apartment. We hoped that living together would help Victoria to get off drugs and get her act together. We shared an apartment from September 2014 until around February 2015.

It didn't work.

I remember coming home from work to find literally hundreds of whippets containers strewn about. Whippets are the small chargers containing nitrous oxide, such as whipped cream cans. People inhale the nitrous oxide, cutting off the oxygen to the brain. The high lasts only for a few minutes—so Victoria would do them over and over.

Before my eyes, Victoria was spiraling further and further down. I felt paralyzed to help her. I tried hiding her diary and getting her out of the apartment. Nothing seemed to help.

One day in February 2015, I came home to an empty apartment. Victoria had moved all of her things out. She only left behind my hair straightener that she had borrowed—and a note. I remember that her note said, "I'm not happy. I feel like my life revolves around you. I need to focus on myself now. I'm not mad at you, and I hope you won't be mad at me either."

Victoria moved back home.

I was so very upset that she left without talking to me. Without even saying goodbye.

After that, we drifted apart. I moved out of the apartment. It was just too sad to live there alone. I got my own place. Over the next month or two, Victoria and I texted back and forth a bit. I missed my friend.

In late May 2015, Victoria reached out to me. We met at the Thrift Mart, which her mom owns.

We talked for hours. Victoria excitedly told me that she had gone to rehab and met a guy. She told me that she hadn't even had a glass of wine since rehab—let alone drugs. She confessed that her boyfriend had done heroin a few times. Then she contradicted herself, admitting that she had tried it too. I knew that her new boyfriend was not good for her.

Victoria and I left the Thrift Mart, and we went to Starbucks. I took her to my new apartment, and we hung out there for a bit. I tried to convince her to sleep over, but she said she wanted to go to her boyfriend's. This struck me as very odd. It was unusual for her. That was the first time Victoria ever put a guy ahead of me.

I drove Victoria back to the Thrift Mart. That was the last time I saw her.

Two weeks later, Victoria's received this text from her boyfriend's ex-girlfriend.

> Hi this is _____ His baby momma. I'm here spending the weekend at his house. Feel free to come by and confront him about fucking me tonight and begging me for weeks to come to town so I can suck his dick like he is obsessed with. He's using you for money and he uses the money to shoot up and tell me what a crazy bitch you are and you cut your wrists and he's saved u from killing yourself so many times and he only speaks to you so your family won't ruin his life with legal action. SURPRISE he's a super convincing kniving piece of shit. Oh and he's unconscious on Xanax and heroin right now and that's why I have his phone. Enjoy reading with that. Tata

On June 6, 2015, Victoria Siegel passed away at her home in Windermere. She died from acute methadone and sertraline toxicity, according to the medical examiner's report. Her death was ruled an accident.

Saying Goodbye

*The following pages are transcripts of the heartfelt words
delivered by the Siegel family at Victoria's funeral service.*

Words from David Siegel
at the Service

I haven't even started, but I'm already breaking up. I want to thank you all for turning out and honoring our family today. This is the most horrible thing in my life. I have no script. I'm going to speak from my heart. I don't know if I'm going to get through it. Bear with me.

No parent should have to go through this. Walking down the aisle a few minutes ago. I should have been walking her down the aisle. That's what parents are supposed to do. It should have been me lying there, not her. I'm sorry.

She was a wonderful girl. She was a beautiful little girl, and she grew into a beautiful big girl. But she was troubled, like so many other teens today are troubled. She found comfort in taking prescription drugs when she couldn't handle things. And she also got herself off of them voluntarily as well just a month ago. She fell in love for the first time in her life—to the wrong person. At her most vulnerable, she got a horrible cyberattack from his ex-girlfriend that put her over the top. It was on the 30-day anniversary of the time they met.

We don't know if Victoria did it on purpose or if it was accidental. We were out of town. Today she was supposed to have been on a cruise with her family. Instead we're laying her to rest. It's not the way it's supposed to happen.

But this is not about celebrating Victoria. One of the reasons we had an open casket was that every one of you will leave here with an impression in your head and say, "That's not going to be my child." We have such an epidemic in this country of our children getting on drugs. Over six children every single day overdose on drugs just in this community. We're going to celebrate Victoria's legacy by starting the Victoria Siegel Foundation (a.k.a. the Victoria's Voice Foundation). It's going to keep other children from ending up where she is today. We'll get over this grief. But her legacy is going to be that other children will live as a result of her losing her life.

We're going to speak at schools and build a facility like the Betty Ford facility where kids can come who are troubled. Parents can bring their children. It's not going to cost them an arm and a leg. We put on the invitation today that in lieu of flowers if you want to make a donation to the Victoria Siegel Foundation, that's what we want. We don't need your money; we need your support. When you invest money in something, it makes you a supporter.

This isn't going to take the Siegel family. It will take a village. A village of people right here. We have to put an end to this so other families aren't suffering like we are.

We also want you to leave here and go home and hug your children tighter than ever before. Hug your grandchildren. Be thankful that you have them. We as a family are stronger now than we have ever been.

Words from Jackie Siegel

Good afternoon and thank you all for coming and for your loving support. It really means a lot at this very difficult time for us.

Victoria, my God, she was so hardheaded. You know, she just wouldn't listen to me, and it's tough as a parent. But we were getting closer, and just yesterday we were supposed to leave on a cruise—me, Victoria, and the children. I was going to do special Mommy time with her, and she was so excited. She went and renewed her passport and paid $375 to overnight it. That's her passport photo up there, which turned out so beautiful. I'm wearing the earrings she was wearing for the photo. She didn't have any intentions of doing this to herself. I believe it was an accident, and she thought she was going to wake up the next day.

And gosh, some of the things she used to irritate me with are what I'm going to miss the most. Like when she raided my closet, and my clothes were disappearing, especially my underwear. I was yelling at the lady who cleans my clothes. I thought I had a stalker or something! Then I found out it was her.

We were sent a poem the other day by Mrs. World April Lufriu when she heard of Victoria's passing. It's called "Sweet Child."

God made a sweet child,
a child who never grew old.
He made a smile of sunshine.
He molded a heart of pure gold. He made that child as close
to an angel as anyone can ever be.
God made that child
and He gave that child to me.
Then God saw His wonderful creation growing very tired
and weak,
so He wrapped the child in his loving arms and said,
"You my child, I keep."
But now my sweet child is an angel,
free from hurt and pain.
I love you forever
until we meet again.
So many times I've missed you,
so many times I've cried.
If all my love could have saved you,
sweet child you would have never died.

Even all of the money in the world couldn't save her. I know David would give up his entire fortune…

One of the things I'm going to miss about Victoria is hearing that little tone in her voice when she said, "I love you, Momma." And I'm going to miss her saying, "I love you, Daddy."

I'm going to miss her so much.

Words from David Siegel Jr.

Rikki had a peaceful, young, beautiful soul.

One thing she loved was to make other people happier. She would go out of her way to think of others before herself. She just loved to see other people happy.

I remember the last thing that she gave me was this purple shirt, and when she showed it to me, I told her I loved it! Seeing that smile on her face. It was so gorgeous—as bright as the sun in the sky.

Words from Daniel Siegel

Victoria Elizabeth Siegel—that was her name, but we called her Rikki. She chose that name because she thought it suited her personality.

Regardless of how wealthy her background was, she was not afraid to pave her own path. She did things her way and only her way.

Some of you knew her as little  Victoria, our mommy's first child. To us, she was much more than a big sister. In my eyes, she was a goddess and will remain one for all eternity. She had a beautiful soul that can never be replaced.

Words from Debbie Siegel

I always looked up to Rikki. Everything she did, I would always copy her. Rikki was a happy person. She did everything for everyone else. No matter who you were or what you did, she didn't care. She only looked at the good.

Words from Drew Siegel

As we sit here today, many of you think that Victoria, otherwise known as Rikki, is gone. But to me, her beautiful soul is standing at the back of the room, watching over all of us.

Rikki was not like anyone you've met before. She was free and anxious to explore new things. Aside from dogs, Rikki loved watching movies, painting, drawing, and cooking. She was very good at music, and writing, and she also loved photography. I also remember how good she was at hide-and-seek. I want to pretend this is one of those games where she found the best hiding spot.

Words from Jordan Siegel

I know that everyone is sad that we won't get to see Rikki anymore, but I know one day we will get to see her again. I also feel sad knowing that my big sister had to go through so much pain, but now she lives in everlasting peace in paradise, where there is no more pain or sadness.

Words from Jacqueline Siegel

One of my favorite memories of Rikki is when she taught me how to snowboard. I have a feeling that she is watching us from a better place, and she is at peace. Even though she is not here, she's always going to be in our hearts.

Words from Jonquil Siegel

Rikki made everybody a happy person just by looking at you. She had this smile you could see from miles away. The way she talked to you made you think the world was a better place.

Final Words
from David Siegel

Victoria was the perfect storm.

She was a bright, creative, and artistic young woman, who started down a dangerous path of addiction.

She had anxieties and didn't know what she wanted to do with her life. So we sent her to a psychiatrist, who prescribed drugs. It was the beginning of the end of Victoria's life.

We miss her every second of every day.

A Guide to
Abused Substances

It's shockingly simple for teens and even young children to discover ways to get high. Still, even the savviest parents are liable to be stunned by some of the substances their kids are using to alter their consciousness.

It is harder than ever these days to protect kids from drug-promoting influences. According to the American Academy of Pediatrics, the media is a key driver of adolescent substance abuse. The two most significant drug threats to our kids? Alcohol and tobacco. And that should come as no surprise because billions of dollars are spent advertising these substances.

It's not just the advertising that hooks kids. Movies with R and PG-13 ratings that depict movie stars enjoying a smoke or drink—or drugs—make these substances highly appealing to young people. Then there's all of the other media that comes to our kids on screens of all sizes.

Beyond tobacco and alcohol, other mind-altering substances are highly addictive and can be deadly. These include over-the-counter products such as antihistamines, prescription drugs like depressants and opioids, and of course illegal drugs such as amphetamines and heroin.

But as dangerous for young people as many of these substances are, simply acquiring them is also dangerous. These acts can put a young person at risk for arrest—or worse. The truth is, illegal drugs often put kids in the company of criminals. At that point, children may become vulnerable to other dangers, including sexual exploitation and breaking the law.

We consulted the United States Drug Enforcement Administration, the National Institute on Drug Abuse (NIDA), and other expert sources for the following crucial facts.

Over-the-Counter Substances

ALCOHOL

Street names: Sauce, juice, hooch, booze, brew

What it is: Alcohol depresses the central nervous system. It affects the areas of the brain that control the body's respiration, heart rate, and consciousness. In extreme cases of heavy drinking, alcohol can turn off those parts of the brain and cause a coma or death.

Forms: Beer, wine, and liquor such as vodka, gin, rum, tequila, and brandy

Stats: It's not surprising to hear that alcohol use is common among teens and college-age kids. As many as 80 percent of kids in high school have tried an alcoholic drink, according to Nemours. More than 4,300 adolescents under age 21 die from alcohol each year, data from the Centers for Disease Control and Prevention found.

Signs of abuse: One obvious telltale sign of using alcohol is a hangover. Headache, nausea, vomiting, and feeling shaky can come on 8 to 12 hours after drinking. Other signs of alcohol abuse include a lack of coordination, changes in perception and emotions, poor judgment, risky behaviors, and bad breath.

Signs of overdose: People who have alcohol poisoning may vomit, have slowed breathing, they pass out, and they are difficult to wake up.

Other facts: Drinking during the teen years has major effects on kids' developing brains. One study gave teenagers a cognitive test before drinking began and then six years later. Researchers discovered that the kids who started drinking alcohol weekly at earlier ages performed poorly in memory tests.

NICOTINE

Brand name: JUUL, an e-cigarette device that looks like a computer flash drive and has become a favorite among kids

What it is: Nicotine is a highly addictive chemical. Cigarettes have been the traditional vehicle to deliver the drug, but young people are now turning to e-cigarettes, or vaping, which combines nicotine with sweet flavors. Tobacco products are also considered a gateway drug to more dangerous drugs, such as cocaine.

Forms: E-cigarettes, vaporizers, or tobacco, which can be smoked, chewed, or sniffed

Stats: In 2016, 37.8 million adults in the United States smoked cigarettes, and 9 in 10 began before age 18, according to the Centers for Disease Control and Prevention. About 2 in 100 middle school students and 8 in 100 high school students smoked cigarettes in 2016. However, the numbers are higher for e-cigarettes. The Monitoring the Future study conducted by the National Institute on Drug Abuse (NIDA) found that 35.8 percent of 12th graders had tried vaping.

Signs of abuse: Withdrawal symptoms when trying to quit, such as sleep disturbances, eating more, irritability, trouble focusing, and cravings.

Signs of overdose: It is rare but possible to overdose on nicotine, especially for young children. Nicotine poisoning causes trouble breathing, vomiting, headache, weakness, change in heart rate, or fainting.

Other facts: When nicotine hits the bloodstream, the body releases adrenaline, which increases blood pressure and heart rate and causes faster breathing. It also works on the brain to crave more nicotine. Smoking tobacco can lead to chronic bronchitis, emphysema, and cancer.

Over-the-Counter Medications

ANTI-DIARRHEAL DRUGS

Brand name: Imodium

What it is: Drugs that treat diarrhea contain loperamide, which acts like an opioid when it's taken in large amounts. Loperamide can help relieve withdrawal symptoms in people who are addicted to opioids and can cause feelings of euphoria in high doses.

Forms: Liquid, tablets, and capsules

Stats: Abuse of this drug seems to be increasing. A study found that calls to the Texas Poison Center Network almost doubled from 2009 to 2015, and a third of the calls involved teens and young adults. About 18 percent of the cases involved serious heart problems.

Signs of abuse: Fainting, stomach pain, constipation, eye changes, an erratic heartbeat, and loss of consciousness. It can also cause problems with the kidneys.

Signs of overdose: People have died from overdose after taking 100 capsules of loperamide.

ANTIHISTAMINES

Brand name: Benadryl

What it is: Antihistamine allergy drugs contain diphenhydramine.

Forms: Tablets, capsules, and liquid

Signs of abuse: Feelings of light-headedness, poor coordination, a very dry nose and mouth, lack of an appetite, blurry vision, disorientation, drowsiness, stomach problems, temporary erectile dysfunction in men, insomnia, nervousness, hallucinations, visual and aural distortions, and muscle relaxation.

Signs of overdose: Drowsiness, dilated pupils, fever, flushing, dry skin, delirium, hallucinations, convulsions, and a high body temperature. High doses can cause an irregular heartbeat, heart palpitations, loss of consciousness, low blood pressure, or cardiac arrest.

Other facts: Taking the normal dose of antihistamines with pain medicine or decongestants can cause an overdose.

Prescription Drugs

ANABOLIC STEROIDS

Street names: Juice, gym candy, pumpers, andro, stackers

What it is: Anabolic steroids are synthetic versions of the male sex hormone testosterone. Officially, they're known as anabolic-androgenic steroids, or AAS for short. (*Anabolic* refers to muscle building, and *androgenic* relates to increased male sexual characteristics.)

Doctors may prescribe these drugs for legitimate medical reasons. But they are also abused by people who want to increase the size of their muscles or improve their athletic performance or physical appearance.

Forms: People can take anabolic steroids orally or inject them directly into their muscles. The drugs also come as creams or gels that you apply to the skin. "Street" doses can be 10 to 100 times stronger than medically prescribed doses.

Stats: In 2014, *Medical Daily* reported that teen steroid use had doubled between 2012 and 2013. The article also reported that one in five teens knows at least one friend who uses steroids. According to a study from the Partnership for Drug-Free Kids, 11 percent of teens have abused anabolic steroids at least once in their lifetime.

Signs of abuse: Severe acne and changes in sex characteristics (shrunken testicles in males; hair growth in women) may occur.

Signs of overdose: Heart disease, liver problems, stroke, infectious diseases, depression, and suicide can arise from steroid abuse.

Other facts: Unlike some of the other drugs mentioned here, people don't get "high" from taking steroids. But using them for a long time can affect the brain's chemicals—including dopamine and serotonin—just as other drugs can. So over time, they can seriously impact mood and behavior. A person may experience unstable moods and fly off the handle, which is a phenomenon known as 'roid rage.

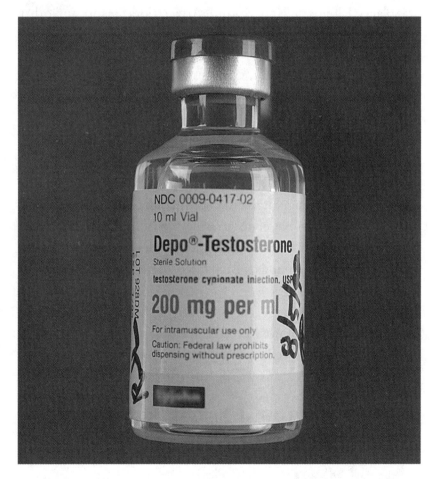

DEPRESSANTS

Street names: Downers, major tranquilizers, antipsychotics, benzos, barbs, candy, phennies, reds, red birds, sleeping pills, tooies, tranks, yellows, yellow jackets

What it is: Depressant drugs include tranquilizers, sedatives, and hypnotics that are usually used to treat anxiety and sleep problems. They include the prescription drugs Valium (diazepam), Xanax (alprazolam), Klonopin (clonazepam), Ativan (lorazepam), and other anti-anxiety medications, along with sleeping pills such as Ambien and Lunesta.

Forms: Pills or capsules (that may be swallowed or crushed) or liquid

Stats: According to the Monitoring the Future study done in 2017, 7.5 percent of 12th graders had used a tranquilizer.

Signs of abuse: Struggling with coordination, memory problems, poor judgment, trouble concentrating, confusion, fatigue, dizziness, lower pulse or breathing rate, lower blood pressure, slurred speech, fever, dilated pupils, visual disturbances, disorientation, or inability to urinate

Signs of overdose: Slowed breathing that could lead to death, or hypoxia, in which not enough oxygen reaches the brain and brain damage occurs

Other facts: Combining these drugs with alcohol can severely slow the heart rate and breathing and cause death.

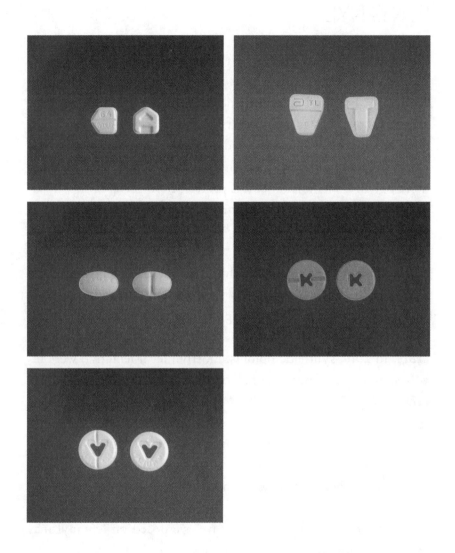

FENTANYL

Street names: Apache, China girl, dance fever, Tango & Cash

What it is: Fentanyl is a synthetic (man-made) opioid. It is in the same class of drugs as heroin and pain medications such as oxycodone, hydrocodone, codeine, and morphine, to name a few. Fentanyl is 30 to 50 times more potent than heroin and 50 to 100 times more potent than morphine. It is prescribed for people who are already taking opioids to relieve chronic or breakthrough pain, such as cancer pain.

Forms: Fentanyl is quickly evolving on the drug landscape, and new forms frequently appear on the "market." It can be injected, snorted, taken in a pill, or even spiked onto blotter paper.

Stats: In 2016, synthetic opioids, mostly illegal fentanyl, were involved in nearly 50 percent of all opioid-related deaths—up 14 percent since 2010.

Signs of abuse: The signs that a person is abusing fentanyl are similar to abuse signs of other opioids—euphoria, drowsiness, nausea, confusion, and extreme relaxation.

Signs of overdose: People who have overdosed on fentanyl may experience slowed breathing—or they may even stop breathing. They may lose consciousness, fall into a coma, or die.

Call 911 if you suspect someone may have overdosed on fentanyl.

OPIOIDS

Street names: Codeine goes by Captain Cody, cody, purple drank, pancakes and syrup, schoolboy, sizzurp, fours and doors, and lean.

Fentanyl is called Apache, China girl, China white, dance fever, friend, and goodfella, among other names.

Hydrocodone goes by vike and Watson-387.

Methadone goes by amidone, fizzies, and chocolate chip cookies.

Oxycodone goes by O.C., oxycet, oxycotton, oxy, hillbilly heroin, and percs.

What it is: Legal prescription pain pills such as codeine, hydrocodone, oxycodone, and others (along with the illegal drug heroin) fall into the category of opioids. These drugs are effective for relieving pain, but they are addictive and can cause a feeling of euphoria, making people want to seek out more and more of them. Easy access also contributes to opioid abuse.

Forms: Tablets, capsules, powder, skin patches, colored chunks, liquid, syrups, suppositories, and lollipops. They're taken orally, smoked, sniffed, or injected.

Stats: Prescription drugs are the most commonly used drugs among 12th graders (after alcohol, marijuana, and tobacco). According to the NIDA's 2017 Monitoring the Future study, 4.2 percent of 12th graders had taken opioid pills in the previous year. In 2015, nearly 35,000 people died of an overdose that involved opioids.

Signs of abuse: Slurred speech, mood swings, lack of motivation and not meeting responsibilities, drowsiness and sleeping more or less often, anxiety, lack of coordination, slower breathing, nausea, vomiting, constipation, agitation, irritability, or depression

Signs of overdose: Small pupils, extreme drowsiness or can't be woken, slow breathing, irregular pulse, or vomiting

Note: The prescription drug naloxone can reverse an opioid drug overdose. Naloxone is a medicine that can treat an opioid overdose on the spot when given immediately. Sometimes, it takes more than one dose to get a person breathing again. Learn more about this lifesaving drug at **DrugAbuse.gov/related-topics/opioid-over-dose-reversal-naloxone-narcan-evzio.**

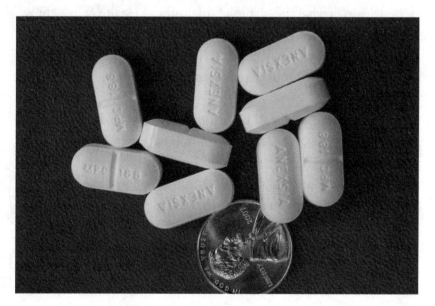

Illegal Drugs

AMPHETAMINES/METHAMPHETAMINES

Street names: Chalk, crystal, ice, meth, and speed

What it is: These two stimulants are closely related and have similar effects. Crystal methamphetamine is so-called because it looks like shards of crystal or shiny, bluish-white rocks. Its "cousin," amphetamine, is a drug used to treat attention-deficit/hyperactivity disorder (ADHD) and narcolepsy, a sleep disorder.

Forms: Methamphetamine can be smoked, inhaled, swallowed as a pill, snorted, or dissolved and injected. The "high" from both drugs comes on fast and fades fast, which leads people to take repeated doses in what the National Institutes of Health calls a "binge and crash" pattern. Some people fall into patterns called "runs," during which they stop eating and sleeping while they keep taking the drug. This dangerous pattern can last for days.

Stats: According to the 2012 National Survey on Drug Use and Health (NSDUH), more than 12 million people (4.7 percent of the population) have tried methamphetamine at least once. NSDUH also reports that approximately 1.2 million people used methamphetamine in the year leading up to the survey.

Signs of abuse: Even tiny amounts of methamphetamine cause serious effects, similar to those of other stimulants, including cocaine and amphetamine. Look for:

Increased wakefulness and physical activity

Heartbeat irregularities

Little or no appetite

Increased body temperature and blood pressure

Breathing faster

Signs of overdose: Methamphetamine overdose can result in a stroke, heart attack, or organ problems.

Other facts: When people use methamphetamine over a long period of time, especially if they inject it, they place themselves at risk for contracting infectious diseases, such as HIV and hepatitis B and C. That's because these diseases are spread through contact with blood or other bodily fluids.

Being high on meth can alter your judgment and lead to bad decision-making and risky behaviors, such as unprotected sex, which increases your chances of acquiring a sexually transmitted disease.

Long-term meth use also leads to these serious consequences:

Extreme weight loss

Sleeping problems

Severe dental problems ("meth mouth")

Violent behavior

Paranoia (extreme and unreasonable distrust of others)

Intense itching, leading to sores from scratching

Anxiety

Hallucinations (sensations and images that seem real but aren't)

Confusion

BATH SALTS

Street names: Bath salts are often sold in little plastic or foil packages tagged as "not for human consumption." Labels may read "bath salts," "plant food," "jewelry cleaner," or "phone screen cleaner."

What it is: Synthetic cathinones, aka "bath salts," are synthetic stimulants related to cathinone, a substance found in the khat plant. In East Africa and Southern Arabia, some people chew khat leaves to get a mild stimulant effect. The artificial versions can be far stronger than khat and can also be quite dangerous.

Health officials call synthetic cathinones "new psychoactive substances (NPS)." These unregulated mind-altering drugs have no legitimate medical use and are made to mimic the effects of controlled substances. Marketers continually reintroduce these substances under new names in an effort to skirt law enforcement attempts to stem their sale.

People typically smoke, snort, or swallow synthetic cathinones.

Forms: Bath salts are typically sold as white or brown crystal-like powders.

Stats: The good news is that these dangerous drugs have not become popular among young people, according to the Drug Policy Alliance in New York City. Bath salts triggered a high of 2,697 calls to poison control centers in 2012. By 2015, the number of calls was 522.

Signs of abuse: People using bath salts may feel paranoid, seem very sociable, have an increased sex drive, experience hallucinations, and have panic attacks. Deaths have been reported from using bath salts.

Note: Do not confuse the drug with Epsom salts, which is a perfectly safe product sold in drug and beauty stores as an additive to the bath.

COCAINE

Street names: Coke, big C, blow

What it is: Made from the leaves of the coca plant native to South America, cocaine is a potent, highly addictive stimulant. This illegal drug resembles a fine, white powder. Dealers may mix it with other substances, such as cornstarch, or with the stimulant amphetamine.

Forms: Cocaine can be snorted through the nose, usually through a straw or a rolled-up bill. It can also be dissolved in water and injected through a hypodermic needle.

Stats: In 2015, nearly 7,000 people died from cocaine overdoses, according to the National Institute on Drug Abuse for Teens.

Signs of abuse: Using cocaine regularly—aka becoming addicted to it—can result in weight loss and malnourishment. People who snort the drug may have frequent nosebleeds or a runny nose. They may become irritable, have trouble sleeping, and become paranoid. In severe cases, they could hallucinate.

Signs of overdose: You can overdose and die the very first time you take cocaine—or unexpectedly any time after that. Drinking alcohol when you're taking cocaine magnifies the danger of overdosing. Problems from overdosing that lead to death or serious injury include heart problems, including irregular heart rhythms and heart attacks, as well as strokes and seizures.

Other facts: Because repeated cocaine use leads to long-term changes in the brain's reward system, cocaine has a very high rate of addiction. After you use it for a while, you require more and more cocaine to achieve the same pleasurable effects. While you're taking cocaine, your normal brain communication is disrupted, due to levels of dopamine becoming higher in the brain circuits that control pleasure and movement. The surge of dopamine interferes with your normal function and causes the "high" of cocaine.

GHB

Street names: G, liquid G, goop, liquid ecstasy, liquid x, grievous bodily harm, Georgia home boy, soap, scoop

What it is: GHB, a depressant usually used to treat narcolepsy, has been used as a date rape drug. It's also considered a club drug. GHB can bring on a feeling of euphoria.

Forms: Liquid or white powder that is added to drinks

Stats: The Monitoring the Future study from 2017 found that 0.4 percent of 12th graders had used GHB in the last year.

Signs of abuse: Slurred speech, euphoria, impulsive behavior, and drowsiness.

Signs of overdose: Drowsiness, lack of motor control, agitation, seizures, nausea, vomiting, a slower heart rate, lower body temperature, slower breathing, seizures, unconsciousness, coma, and death.

Other facts: Combining the drug with alcohol causes even more sedation, breathing problems, and nausea.

INHALANTS

Street names: Inhaling fumes can be called sniffing, snorting, bagging, or huffing. Gases that are inhaled are called laughing gas or whippets. Nitrites are called poppers or snappers.

What it is: The substances in aerosol sprays, gases, and some drugs are mind-altering when they're inhaled, although the high lasts only a few minutes. They cause a feeling of light-headedness and can cause hallucinations or delusions.

Forms: Household products such as paint thinner, gasoline, lighter fluid, glue, markers, spray paints, deodorant spray, vegetable oil spray, or aerosol cleaning products. Nitrite drugs that treat chest pain and anesthesia drugs such as nitrous oxide, ether, and chloroform are also used.

Stats: Among children age 12 to 17, 8.3 percent had used inhalants in their lifetime, the National Survey on Drug Use and Health (NSDUH) found in 2016.

Signs of abuse: Slurred speech, euphoria, dizziness, trouble with coordination, hallucinations, and delusions.

Signs of overdose: Seizures, coma, sudden sniffing death (when the heart stops as a result of inhaling), or suffocation if inhalation is done with a bag or in a small space. If done over and over, inhaling can cause vomiting, drowsiness, or an hours-long headache. Doing it long-term can cause kidney damage, spasms, delayed development, and brain damage.

HEROIN

Street names: Smack, big H, horse, thunder

What it is: Heroin is a highly addictive opioid drug made from morphine, which comes from the opium poppy plant native to Southeast and Southwest Asia, Mexico, and Colombia. It's sold as a white or brown powder, or as a sticky "black tar" substance.

Forms: People inject, sniff, snort, or smoke heroin. Some people mix it with crack cocaine, a practice called speedballing.

Stats: As many as 5,794,000 children between the ages of 12 and 17 have used heroin, according to a 2015 study published in the Centers for Disease Control and Prevention's *Morbidity and Mortality Weekly Report*. According to a CNN report, "The rate of drug overdose deaths involving heroin for this age group in 2015 was one for every 100,000 teens. That's three times what it was in 1999, when the rate was 0.3 overdose deaths for every 100,000."

Signs of abuse: Heroin use is associated with these signs in teenagers:

- Lower than usual grades or unusual poor school performance
- Missing school or extracurricular activities
- Getting into trouble at school
- Changes in personality— becoming hostile, uncooperative, moody, or breaking rules
- Running into trouble with the authorities
- Decreased interest in favorite activities
- Dropping old friends and making new ones
- Demands for privacy

Signs of overdose: The key sign of a heroin overdose is reduced or stopped breathing. Look for shallow breaths, gasping, and very pale, blue-tinted skin. Call 911 immediately if you suspect someone has overdosed with heroin.

KETAMINE

Street names: Special K, K, vitamin K, kit kat, super C, jey, cat valium, green, super acid

What it is: Ketamine is an anesthetic used by veterinarians that makes people feel detached from reality. It causes hallucinations and has been used as a date rape drug because it can make it hard to move. It is also considered a club drug.

Forms: Liquid or white powder that can be swallowed, injected, snorted, or smoked with cigarettes.

Stats: A Monitoring the Future Study from 2017 found that 1.2 percent of 12th graders had used ketamine in the previous year.

Signs of abuse: Numbness, memory and attention problems, hallucinations, sedation, being in a dreamlike state, confusion, high blood pressure, slowed breathing, and unconsciousness.

Signs of overdose: Trouble breathing, nausea, vomiting, chest pain, an irregular heartbeat, high blood pressure, extreme sedation, loss of consciousness, paralysis, violence, terrors, seizures, and coma.

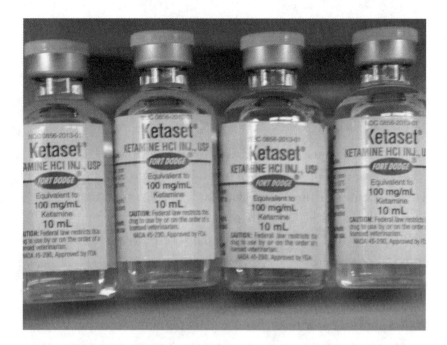

Other facts: Hallucinations are common on ketamine, but high doses can cause an out-of-body experience, which drug users refer to as "going down the K-hole." Taking the drug long-term can cause bladder ulcers, kidney problems, stomach pain, depression, and memory loss.

MARIJUANA

Street names: Boom, bud, chronic, gangster, ganja, grass, herb, kif, Mary Jane, MJ, pot, reefer, skunk, and weed

What it is: Marijuana is the dried leaves and flowers of the *Cannabis sativa* or *Cannabis indica* plant. It is grown in many different concentrations, including sinsemilla, hashish, and extracts. Marijuana is laced with hundreds of plant chemicals, including THC (delta-9-tetrahydrocannabinol), which is responsible for the drug's mind-altering effects.

Forms: Some people smoke marijuana in hand-rolled cigarettes called joints. People may also use glass pipes or water pipes called bongs. Blunts are slit-open cigars that smokers stuff with marijuana.

Some people use vaporizers so they don't have to inhale smoke. These devices pull the active ingredients, including THC, from the marijuana into the vapor. Other vaporizers use marijuana in a liquid extract form. Finally, marijuana can be brewed into beverages or baked into food, such as brownies or cookies.

Stats: According to the National Institute on Drug Abuse for Teens, no reports have ever directly linked marijuana to death, nor are there any reports of people fatally overdosing on marijuana. However, marijuana is often a "gateway drug" to harder drugs. In addition, high concentrations of THC can make some people have hallucinations, attacks of paranoia, and other uncomfortable physical and psychological symptoms.

Smoking marijuana can lead to dangerous inattention while you're behind the wheel. Kids who smoke marijuana tend to get lower grades in school and may even drop out prematurely.

As of 2017, according to the National Institute on Drug Abuse:

0.8 percent of 8th graders
2.9 percent of 9th graders
5.9 percent of 12th graders

…are mostly steady, daily marijuana users.

Signs of abuse: Look for a loss of coordination, being unbalanced, mild to severe sleepiness, or trouble breathing.

Signs of overdose: Kids might unknowingly eat high-potency edible marijuana in candy or baked good form. These edible products contain concentrated marijuana and can cause severe problems. The most common symptoms include rapid heartbeat, dilated pupils, lethargy, and lack of coordination.

Call 911 if you suspect your child may have eaten edible marijuana or is showing symptoms of marijuana overdose.

PCP

Street names: Angel dust, killer weed, rocket fuel, love boat, peace pill, hog, supergrass

What it is: The hallucinogen PCP (phencyclidine) puts people in a trancelike state, making them feel as if they left their bodies. The drug causes numbness in the hands and feet and makes it difficult for people to maintain coordination. It was first used during the 1950s as an anesthetic during surgery, but doctors stopped using it because of its side effects.

Forms: White crystal powder, colored powder, liquid, tablets, and capsules. Liquid and powders are most common and are smoked by placing them on mint, parsley, oregano, tobacco, or marijuana.

Stats: The 2016 National Survey on Drug Use and Health found that 0.2 percent of kids age 12 to 17 had used it.

Signs of abuse: Excessive sweating, a flushed face, nausea, vomiting, eyelids that flicker, disturbed thoughts, and loss of reality.

Signs of overdose: Agitation, aggression, higher body temperature, an irregular heartbeat, high blood pressure, poor coordination or can't control muscles, a catatonic state or hyperactivity, side-to-side eye movements, hallucinations, delusions, unconsciousness, and seizures.

Other facts: A high dose may cause seizures, coma, or death, usually from being injured or from committing suicide while on the drug. Large doses cause symptoms that mimic schizophrenia, interfering with the way people think, causing garbled speech, and making them paranoid and delusional. Mixing PCP with alcohol or anti-anxiety pills is particularly dangerous and raises the risk of a coma.

PSILOCYBIN

Street names: Mushrooms, magic mushrooms, shrooms, caps, little smoke, purple passion

What it is: Psilocybin, the psychedelic compound found in magic mushrooms, causes people to lose track of what is fantasy and what is reality. Sometimes the hallucinations caused by mushrooms are pleasant, while other times a trip may be terrifying. Hallucinations may come back later as a flashback long after taking the drug.

Forms: Dried mushrooms that can be eaten or brewed to make tea

Stats: The Substance Abuse and Mental Health Services Administration survey found that 1.1 percent of kids age 12 to 17 had used mushrooms in 2015.

Signs of abuse: Nervousness, paranoia, nausea.

Signs of overdose: Risky behavior, but risk of death due to overdose is very low.

Other facts: People usually feel sick to their stomach immediately after taking psilocybin and may experience different symptoms based on how potent the mushrooms are, the amount taken, and their mood. If psilocybin is mistaken for another mushroom that's poisonous, it could lead to death.

ROHYPNOL

Street names: Date rape drug, roofie, forget pill, mind eraser, rophies, circles, la rocha, lunch money, roach, and rope, among other names

What it is: Rohypnol is 10 times more potent than the sedative Valium. It has been used to commit date rape. It's also included in the category of club drugs.

Forms: Rohypnol is taken as white or green pills, mixed into drinks, or snorted.

Stats: According to the Monitoring the Future study, 0.6 percent of 8th graders and 0.7 percent of 10th graders had tried Rohypnol.

Signs of abuse: Drowsiness and sleep, amnesia, blackouts, impaired reactions, poor judgment, confusion, slurred speech, or aggression.

Signs of overdose: Sedation, unconsciousness, slow breathing, or a slow heart rate.

Other facts: When it's combined with alcohol, it causes severe sleepiness and even unconsciousness, while a slower heart rate and breathing from the drug can cause death.

STIMULANTS

Street names: Speed, crystal, ice

What it is: Stimulants such as amphetamines are used to treat attention-deficit/hyperactivity disorder (ADHD) and the sleep disorder narcolepsy. They make people feel more energized and focused and can give a feeling of euphoria. They include the prescription drugs Adderall, Dexedrine, and Vyvanse. Illegal drugs such as methamphetamine and ecstasy are also considered amphetamines.

Forms: Pills are swallowed or crushed and snorted.

Stats: About 6 percent of high school seniors had used the stimulant Adderall in the last year, the NIDA's 2017 Monitoring the Future survey found.

Signs of abuse: Weight loss, lower appetite, digestive problems, insomnia, mood swings, aggression, paranoia, anxiety, hallucinations, and trouble keeping up with responsibilities. Methamphetamines can also cause dental issues and skin sores along with a severe drop in weight.

Signs of overdose: Rapid speech, repeating tasks, severe agitation, mental disturbance, hallucinations, paranoia, aggression, violence, compulsive behavior like picking the skin or sniffing, dilated pupils, a higher body temperature, higher heart rate, heart palpitations, chest pain, dehydration, or muscle tremors.

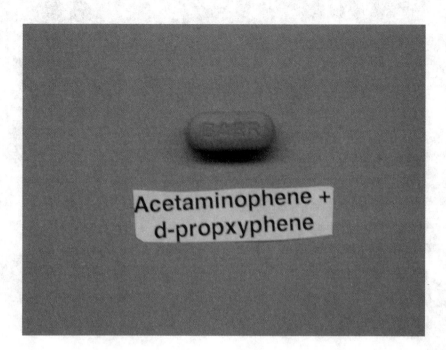

Acetaminophene +
d-propxyphene

Other facts: Studies have found that when young people abuse prescription drugs, they're more likely to become heavy drinkers of alcohol, smoke cigarettes, and use marijuana, cocaine, and other illegal drugs.

How to Prevent Drug Use in Kids

As a parent, you have the power to prevent drug abuse and addiction in your family. The following are research-supported tips from the DEA, the Partnership for Drug-Free Kids, and the Parents Translational Research Center.

Create an overall healthy environment at home. Meeting your child's basic needs by providing healthy foods, a safe home and neighborhood, enough clothing for each season, health care that includes regular medical and dental checkups, and emotional support creates the foundation for a healthy child.

Keep a close relationship during the teen years. Kids who have a supportive relationship with their parents are less likely to use drugs or alcohol. Talk about your interests and ask your kids about theirs. Do activities together, such as going to concerts or exercising; do your best to stay calm when emotions run hot; help your kids through challenges like a fight with a friend; and set a rule that you're honest with each other. Another important step: Give your child some independence while keeping her well-being and safety in mind.

But set boundaries. Being close and supportive is important, but kids of parents who are too lax are also at risk of drug addiction. Set ground rules and stick to them to teach your children responsibility. Be clear that you won't tolerate alcohol use before they turn 21 or any drug use. Set other rules such as curfews and then follow through with consequences if the rules are broken.

Model responsible behavior. If your children see you drinking to excess, using illegal drugs, or abusing prescription drugs, they may follow in your footsteps. The more you expose your kids to drinking, the higher their risk of addiction.

Never share medications. Your medications were prescribed for you. Do not give one family members' medication to another family member—or friend. At best, you're setting a bad example. At worst, a person could be harmed by taking the wrong medication or dosage.

Educate yourself on drugs and signs of drug abuse. You'll better communicate the harmful effects of drugs if you've done some research first. For one, you should know that drugs are more potent today than ever before. Heroin, for instance, is pure, inex-

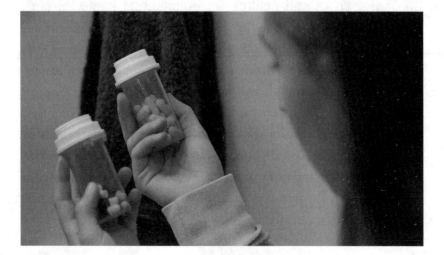

pensive, and frequently laced with the synthetic opioid fentanyl, which is highly potent. You can find an excellent 40-page downloadable booklet by the Drug Enforcement Administration: Growing Up Drug Free: A Parent's Guide to Prevention on their website: https://www.dea.gov/sites/default/files/2018-06/growing-up-drug-free-2017.pdf.

Be able to spot the signs of drug use in your kids. Read our drug guide beginning on page 226 and "How to Spot Drug Use in Kids" on page 271.

Address risk factors early. A family history of drug or alcohol abuse, a mental health issue such as depression or ADHD, a traumatic experience, or problems with impulse control put your child at higher risk of becoming addicted.

Know your kids' friends. Talk to your teen if you have concerns about a friend, and have conversations about healthy friendships. If your child's siblings don't like his friends, consider it a warning sign.

Know your kids' friends' rules. Also ask your teen's friends' parents what their rules are for alcohol use and if they have easy access to alcohol or drugs in their homes.

Pry some more. Connect with your kids on social media and keep track of what they're posting, along with what their friends are posting. Also look for clues in their room. Venture in, clean up, and if you suspect a problem and your teen is not forthcoming, look through their things, including journals.

Pay attention when things go missing. You don't want to believe your child or your child's friends could be responsible when valuables go missing, but you don't want to dismiss the thought and regret it later. Consider missing cash, electronics, jewelry, and especially prescription drugs that don't turn up after a thorough search a major warning sign.

Take tattoos and piercings as a red flag. Of course, not everyone with ink or a nose ring uses drugs, but studies have found that people who get them do tend to be risk-takers. In one study published in the *Journal of the American Academy of Dermatology*, researchers looked at 500 men and women and found an association between tattoos and body piercings and alcohol and drug use, along with jail time.

Be present. Being home and checking in on your teen's get-togethers reinforces with them that an adult is around and they need to be on good behavior. When your teen is away from home, know where he is and whom he's hanging out with.

Open up the conversation. Don't shy away from talking about the risks of drug and alcohol abuse, and listen to your teen's thoughts about it as well. Tell your teen that her brain is still developing and that drugs and alcohol can rewire it to make her particularly vulnerable to addiction.

Share expert resources. The US Drug Enforcement Administration video "Chasing the Dragon: The Life of an Opiate Addict" is available at https://www.dea.gov/galleries/education-and-outreach-videos/chasing-dragon. This powerful 49-minute film shares true experiences of people suffering from drug addiction. You can also find a Chasing the Dragon discussion guide on their site: DEA.gov.

Visit these sites and share them with your kids:

www.justthinktwice.com: Geared toward teens in providing drug awareness/prevention on the dangers of drug abuse.

www.getsmartaboutdrugs.com: Geared toward parents/adults/educators in bringing awareness and education surrounding teen misuse of prescription drugs

www.campusdrugprevention.gov: DEA's latest effort to support drug abuse prevention programs on college campuses and in surrounding communities. The website was created for professionals working to prevent drug abuse among college students, including educators, student health centers, and student affairs personnel. In addition, it serves as a useful tool for college students, parents, and others involved in campus communities.

The Addition Policy Forum created a series of informative, easy-to-understand animated videos that explain what addiction is, risk factors for substance use disorder, and information about treatment. The animated series aims to expand public understanding about addiction and replace the myths and misinformation that keep substance use disorders (SUDs) from being treated like any other medical condition. You can view the videos here: https://www.addictionpolicy.org/addiction-series-main. Watch videos like this with your children.

Have a drug test on hand. We are strong advocates of preventing drug use by doing random drug tests on your kids. If your child knows you test him for drugs or alcohol, he's more likely to say no if it's offered to him. And he has the perfect excuse if his friends are pressuring him.

Buy tests to use at home for alcohol, tobacco, opiates, benzodiazepines, and a wide variety of illicit drugs, such as cocaine and meth. You'll find them at the pharmacy or online, and they range in price from less than $10 to more than $20, depending on the drug being tested. They require a urine sample or a swab of saliva.

Choose the best time to test. Kids who use drugs tend to start during their teenage years, so keep that in mind. Also know that kids are more likely to begin using alcohol during transitions, such as puberty or times of upheaval like divorce. You may want to time a test for the day after a party or after time spent with friends. Certainly, if you see signs of drug use in your child, go ahead and test.

Stock naloxone at home. This won't prevent drug use, but having this powerful opioid antidote on hand can prevent your child's death from an overdose. It's available by prescription and over the counter in most states. In 2016, 10 states required a prescription to get the drug, but laws continue to change to grant greater access. It's stocked behind the counter at drugstores, so you'll have to ask the pharmacist for it if you're buying it over the counter.

Submit to insurance. Without a prescription, Narcan nasal spray costs about $150, according to an article in the *New England Journal of Medicine*. Injectable naloxone cost $39.60. However, the cost of the drug has been on the rise.

Dispose of mediations properly. Unused or expired prescription medications are a public safety issue, leading to potential accidental poisoning, misuse, and overdose. Proper disposal of unused drugs saves lives and protects the environment. Talk with your pharmacist about take-back medication programs. The US Drug Enforcement Administration organizes a national medication take-back day.

If you can't find a take-back site, look for disposal instructions on the medication label. If none are given, follow these steps to throw the drugs in the household trash: Remove the medicine from its original container and mix it with an undesirable substance, such as used coffee grounds or kitty litter. Place the mixture in a sealable bag, empty bag, or other container to prevent medicine from leaking or breaking out of a garbage bag.

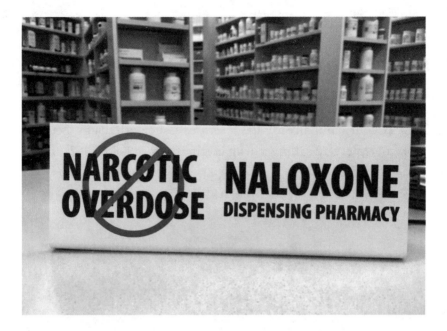

Don't flush medication down the toilet. This can introduce drug residues into rivers, lakes, and community drinking water supplies.

Join Operation Prevention. Talk with your child's school about Operation Prevention. This no-cost program was created by the US Drug Enforcement Administration and Discovery Education. It's a science-based program for students ages 8 to 18 to combat opioid misuse. It's available now in every school, home, and state in the nation to kick-start life-saving actions. The program includes digital classroom lessons, a parent toolkit, and virtual field trips. Visit www.operationprevention.com to learn more.

Get involved in drug prevention and advocacy. As a parent, you have the monumental ability to shape your child's attitude toward drugs. Joining an organization to make a difference locally and around the country is a wonderfully inspiring way to positively influence your children. When your kids see your advocacy work, they'll want to get involved too. As a result, they'll be more informed and energized to fight the drug war along with you.

Getting the information and knowing what to do is the first step. If your child already has a serious issue with drugs, get help from an expert by calling a drug hotline such as 1-800-662-HELP.

How to Spot
Drug Use in Kids

Parents of addicted teens say the signs were there—if they had only paid more attention.

The following are the red flags you need to look for, according to the Partnership for Drug-Free Kids. If your child exhibits a few of them, it doesn't necessarily point to a drug or alcohol problem, but the key is to pay attention and take action if necessary.

If you see enough that makes you concerned, have a conversation with your teen and ask, "Are you drinking or using drugs?" If the answer is yes (or no but you're still worried something is amiss), make an appointment with your child's doctor or a clinical psychologist.

Also keep an eye on signs around the home, such as missing prescriptions, alcohol, cigarettes, or money. Then look out for these signs in your child.

Behavioral changes that may include:

- Breaking curfew
- Avoiding eye contact
- Locking the bedroom door

- Missing school, not completing homework, or losing interest in school, hobbies, or sports
- Having the munchies
- Needing cash
- Using eye drops or nasal sprays frequently
- Chewing gum or using mints often
- Staying out late or disappearing for long periods
- Making phone calls in secret
- Laughing for no reason
- Making excuses
- Losing balance or being clumsy
- Becoming loud and obnoxious
- Having high energy followed by long periods of sleep
- A change in relationship with you, family members, or friends

Personality changes that may include:

- Moodiness, withdrawal, or depression
- Fewer inhibitions
- Becoming quiet and not communicating
- Showing anger and hostility
- Being more secretive or deceitful
- Trouble focusing, difficulty staying motivated, and being hyperactive
- Being uncharacteristically euphoric

Health and hygiene changes that may include:

- Losing or gaining weight
- Smelling like smoke or alcohol, or having bad breath
- Looking messy and not taking care of hygiene
- Extreme fatigue and lethargy
- Getting sick more often, vomiting, or complaining of headaches
- Slurring speech or talking fast
- Red, flushed cheeks and sweating
- Nosebleeds or a runny nose for no reason
- Sores around the mouth or bruises on the body
- Being very thirsty and licking lips

- Marks on arms or legs, and trying to cover them up with long sleeves or pants in warm weather

- Burn marks on hands from cigarettes or joints burning down
- Having more accidents or injuries

Resources

You're not alone. There is a network of organizations and groups in your community that offer assistance. All you have to do is reach out and ask for help.

Victoria's Voice Foundation

Victoria's Voice Foundation has a free Addiction Community Resources toolkit created by Addiction Policy Forum. It includes information on prevention, treatment, recovery, and helplines. You can download it here:

VictoriaSiegelFoundation.org/get-help/resources

> 5601 Windhover Drive
> Orlando, FL 32819
> Phone: 1-800-257-6077
> VictoriaSiegelFoundation.org

Addition Policy Forum

The Addiction Policy Forum is a diverse partnership of organizations, policymakers and stakeholders committed to working together to elevate awareness around addiction and to improve national policy through a comprehensive response that includes prevention, treatment, recovery and criminal justice reform. Their website includes information and videos about addiction.

1101 K Street NW

Suite 1000

Washington, DC 20005

Addictionpolicy.org

American Academy of Addiction Psychiatry

The AAAP's Patient Referral Program will help you find an addiction psychiatrist near you.

400 Massasoit Avenue, Suite 307

East Providence, RI 02914

Phone: 1-401-524-3076

AAAP.org/patient-resources/find-a-specialist

Brent Shapiro Foundation for Drug Prevention

Founded upon personal tragedy, it is the Brent Shapiro Foundation's vision to conquer alcohol and drug dependence by turning the fear, grief, and helplessness caused from this disease into awareness, compassion, and support. The foundation created Save A Life Cards, business cards with critical information about drug overdose. To date, they have given out more than 5,000,000 free cards across the country. To receive Save A Life Cards, email info@ brentshapiro.com with your mailing address and the quantity of cards you would like to receive.

10250 Constellation Boulevard, 18th Floor

Los Angeles, CA 90067

Phone: 310-282-6246

BrentSharpiro.org

Community Anti-Drug Coalitions of America

CADCA has members in every U.S. state and territory and 23 countries around the world. It works to strengthen the capacity of community coalitions to create and maintain safe, healthy, and drug-free communities by providing technical assistance and training, public policy advocacy, media strategies, and marketing programs, training, and special events.

> 625 Slaters Lane, Suite 300
> Alexandria, VA 22314
> Phone: 1-800-54-CADCA
> CADCA.org

National Institute on Drug Abuse (NIDA) for Teens

This website is a project of the National Institute on Drug Abuse (NIDA), National Institutes of Health (NIH), and U.S. Department of Health and Human Services. This site offers information for teens, middle and high school teachers, and parents. Teens can find information on how drugs affect the brain and body, featuring videos, games, blog posts, and more.

> https://teens.drugabuse.gov

Partnership for Drug-Free Kids

Partnership for Drug-Free Kids is a nonprofit organization that supports families who are struggling with a child's substance use. It provides confidential one-on-one support through a hotline and offers support via live chat and e-mail.

> 352 Park Avenue South, 9th Floor
> New York, NY 10010
> Phone: 1-855-DRUGFREE
> Text: 55753
> DrugFree.org

Shatterproof

Shatterproof is a community of advocates, ambassadors, and supporters working to make change to save people's lives. The organization's Substance Use Disorder Treatment Task Force developed the National Principles of Care, a standard for addiction treatment based on research.

135 West 41st Street, 6th Floor

New York, NY 10036

Phone: 1-800-597-2557

Shatterproof.org

Substance Abuse and Mental Health Services Administration

SAMHSA is the Substance Abuse and Mental Health Services Administration. It is a free, confidential, 24/7, 365-day-a-year treatment referral and information service (English and Spanish) for individuals and their families facing mental and/or substance abuse disorders.

The service provides referrals to local treatment facilities, support groups, and community-based organizations. Callers can also order free publications and other information.

5600 Fishers Lane

Rockville, MD 20857

Phone: 1-800-662-HELP (4357) TTY: 1-800-487-4889

SAMHSA.gov

Young People in Recovery

YPR provides recovery support services and connects individuals, families, and communities in recovery. Find local chapters on its website.

150 Oneida Street

Denver, CO 80220

Phone: 1-720-600-4977

YoungPeopleInRecovery.org

United States Drug Enforcement Administration

The Drug Enforcement Adminstration (DEA)'s Community Outreach Section provides the public with current and relevant drug information about illicit drug use, the misuse of prescription drugs, drug use trends, and the health consequences of drug use. The Community Outreach Section also develops drug information brochures, drug fact sheets, pamphlets, and parent/teacher drug education guides to assist the community in identifying drug use and finding help.

Another major component of the Community Outreach Section is collaboration with various drug use prevention partners. These partners include other federal agencies, national and regional prevention organizations, law enforcement organizations, community coalitions, fraternal and civic organizations, youth-serving organizations, state and local governments, and school districts. DEA supports our partners, who present significant opportunities for involvement in prevention efforts by providing drug trend information at local community events as well as at national conferences and professional educational forums.

800 K Street, N.W

Suite 500

Washington, DC 20001

Phone: 202-305-8500

DEA.gov

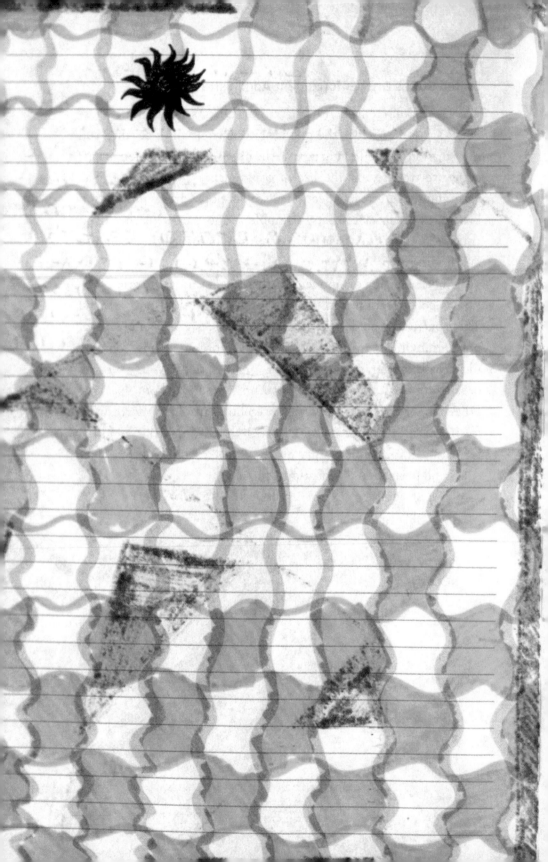

Words of Support

by Kimberly Friedmutter, CHt
Author of *Subconscious Power: Use Your Inner Mind to Create the Life You've Always Wanted*
UCLA Health Systems Board Member at Large

This is a very powerful, original, and personal book that replicates the journal of my good friend Jackie Siegel's daughter, the late Victoria Siegel.

This creative, sweet, and beautiful girl was swept away by a tide of addiction that started innocently enough, with prescribed medication for ADHD and the odd cigarette, escalating into a terrifying roller coaster of prescription and illegal drug dependency.

In these heartbreakingly honest chapters, filled with as much life and laughter as there is despair, we join Victoria as she battles to break the hold the drugs have over her. We are privileged to join her as she travels the world with her family that she so obviously loves and adores.

I don't think I have ever seen such a riveting compilation that speaks to young people about drugs, their hopes and fears for their future, and their struggle to be independent and "cool" while trying to meet the expectations of everyone around them. This book literally speaks to young people in their own language, making it essential reading for children of school age and beyond.

This book is not only unique, bright, and brilliant, just like Victoria herself, but it is full of illuminating insight offered to you, having cost the ultimate price. Victoria's life and legacy will be the gift she now gives you, in these precious pages.

Afterword
by David Siegel

I have built a very successful company, but now my only mission in life is to save lives through the Victoria's Voice Foundation and hopefully prevent other parents from going through what our family has experienced from the death of our beloved daughter.

In 2016, more young people died from overdoses of prescription and street drugs than were killed in the Vietnam War. That's more than 66,000 lives lost to these deadly substances. The death toll is rising each year.

By midnight tonight, another 200 young people will have taken their last breaths. Imagine all of those body bags lined up. It's like a bomb exploding in a busy shopping mall every day. If that was happening, there would be an immediate and intense effort to target the people responsible.

The statistics on teen drug use are staggering: One in six middle schoolers and one in three high schoolers have used marijuana in the past month.

Drug addiction costs our country $442 billion—each year.

President Donald Trump declared the drug epidemic to be a "public health emergency." But little is being done to make Americans aware of the dangers of prescription pain killers and opioids such as heroin and methadone.

Now we are fighting a new generation of the most powerful—and virtually undetectable—chemical weapons that have ever been created—synthetic opioids like fentanyl imported from China. People are dying from just touching these drugs or inhaling them. First responders and nurses have passed out just trying to treat people who have overdosed on these drugs. Dealers are giving away free samples to hook a new generation of drug users.

Many of the kids who are dying are "good kids." They're not high school dropouts or felons. They are kids like our beautiful daughter Victoria. They're kids like yours. They're young, mostly white, educated, and smart. They are often from "good families" and had bright futures ahead of them.

Marijuana: The Gateway Drug

People say marijuana is "safe." They report "no one has died from smoking pot!" Some even assert it's a cure for cancer. It's legal in many states.

Some of these people might be well intentioned, but they are missing a critical fact: Smoking marijuana changes the chemical balance in the brain. People who try it get high, but their brains adapt, and they need more and more to get high. In time, they crave a stronger high.

I do not support legalized medical marijuana because I believe it paves the way for legalized recreational marijuana.

Your Medicine Cabinet: The Dealer in Your Home

You should think of your pill bottles as being as deadly as loaded guns. If you have pills you're no longer taking, get them out of your home. Many pharmacies and police stations have programs to safely dispose of unused medications. Never flush them down the toilet. Treatment companies can't completely filter medications out of our drinking water.

Your Most Powerful Weapon: Drug Testing

Drug test your teens every few months. This is a huge deterrent against them experimenting with drugs. Teenagers often lie, and they are often good at hiding things.

You can buy drug testing kits at pharmacies and variety stores like Walmart. When you tell your teens about testing, you might be surprised by their reactions. They might be relieved. You are putting limits on their behavior, and you are providing them with the perfect reason to give their friends who might offer them drugs: "Oh no, I can't even *try* it. My folks drug test me! I'll be caught for sure!"

Your Last Hope: Naloxone

Right now, today, put this book down and go buy naloxone. This antidote to drug overdose was approved by the Federal Drug Administration in 1971. It's 100 percent safe. It saves lives. But almost no one has heard of it.

The brand name is Narcan. You can buy this nasal spray from your pharmacist without a prescription. Keep one at home, and keep another in your car.

Narcan reverses drug overdose. A person who took too much medication can be lying on the ground, turning blue, and if given Narcan, it buys around 90 minutes of life, potentially enough time to get them to an emergency department.

After taking an overdose, Victoria was found with a faint pulse. But first responders didn't have Narcan to save her.

This has weighed on my mind. Had Victoria been given Narcan, I believe that she would still be alive today.

Hope you never need Narcan, but have it on hand just in case.

Our Advocacy

On June 6, 2015, we received the call that no parent should ever have to get. Our beautiful, vibrant daughter Victoria had died of a drug overdose.

We could have crawled into bed, pulled the covers over our heads, and become basket cases. Instead we decided that we were going to do whatever it takes to prevent this from happening to other parents.

Since losing our daughter Victoria, we have worked passionately to help end the drug abuse epidemic. Not a day goes by without us working to further this goal.

We started our journey in Washington, D.C. Through a Congressman friend, we met with the Surgeon General of the United States, Vivek Murphy. We also met with the acting director of operations of the Drug Enforcement Administration. We literally walked the halls of Congress, enlisting the help of many Senators and Representatives. We toured the DEA Museum, which gave us valuable insight into the drug abuse epidemic.

We met with top drug experts, such as Mark Gold and Miriam Adelson. We visited numerous rehabs, such as Hazeldon Betty

Ford, Rivermend, and Georgia Detox and attended counseling sessions with heroin and cocaine addicts. We went to drug rallies on the Capitol, and we attended and sponsored drug seminars. We corresponded with other like-minded people who were working on the epidemic. We met with public schools, private schools, and state universities. We talked to dozens of addicts and their families, and we read all we could find about the horrible drug epidemic.

We are proud to share the following actions and accomplishments that we have made to date.

Victoria's Voice Foundation: We started our foundation in Victoria's honor to save lives so we don't lose our future generations to drug abuse and addiction.

Letter to President Elect: In November 2016, we penned a letter to then-President Elect Trump urging him to focus on the drug problem here in the United States.

CARA Act: Through the Victoria's Voice Foundation, we played a pivotal role in Congress passing the Comprehensive Addiction and Recovery Act on July 22, 2016. It was signed into law by President Barack Obama. CARA is starting to make a difference by transforming the way the federal government treats addiction and ensuring that federal resources are devoted to evidence based prevention, treatment, and recovery programs that work. CARA also provided law enforcement new tools to reverse overdoses, and it is helping communities respond to the heroin and opioid epidemic.

Victoria Siegel Controlled Substance Education and Awareness Act: We were instrumental in passage of the Victoria Siegel Controlled Substance Education and Awareness Act, along with local elected officials, which provides statutory language to allow for future controlled substance addiction support and treatment resources, telephone helplines and website links that provide counseling and emergency assistance for individuals dealing with substance abuse, and encouragement of collaboration between agencies, organizations, and institutions to create a systematic approach to increasing public awareness regarding controlled substance safety.

Florida House Bills: We offered our strong support for the successful passage of several pieces of legislation in Florida that have done a number of things, including requiring prescribers who are authorized to prescribe opioids to complete a 2-hour training course every 2 years. It also requires limitation on how many days prescribers can prescribe a controlled substance. And it created a greater emphasis on the Prescription Drug Monitoring Program.

Heroin Task Force: We have been part of the Orange County Florida Heroin Task Force since it was formed.

Shatterproof: To raise awareness about the drug abuse epidemic, Jackie rappelled off of one of the tallest buildings in Los Angeles during a Shatterproof event.

Naloxone: This drug was discovered 46 years ago. It's FDA approved and 100 percent safe. It reverses a drug overdose. Very few police officers and first responders carry it. Up until 2016, no police officer in Central Florida had carried it but now due to our efforts, they all carry it and are saving lives every day. One police officer told David that if he had to leave one item home he would rather leave his gun vs. his Naloxone, because the Naloxone will save more lives than his gun.

Mrs. America Pageant: Fighting drug abuse has become the main cause supported by the Mrs. America Pageant. This also helps to make the 50 Mrs. America contestants advocates who help to educate more people about the opioid epidemic.

Speaking: We have spoken before Congress. We have also spoken to hundreds of thousands of people all across the United States. David spoke to more than 15,000 Liberty University students, bringing them to their feet. His presentation was broadcast to millions of people.

Positive things are happening. We invite you to join us in our fight to end the drug abuse epidemic. We dream of building a clinic someday where people could come to recover from their addictions.

If you'd like us to speak at your community, to your schools, or to your organizations, reach out to us at contact@victoriasvoicebook.com or to our publisher at jenniferreich@momosapublishing.com.

Our goal is to save as many lives as possible.

About the Victoria's Voice Foundation

Victoria, a dreamer with a tremendous heart, was the oldest of seven kids and liked her parents to call her Rikki. She was a recent high school graduate when she tragically died from a drug overdose on June 6, 2015, at age 18.

Victoria was one of 129 Americans to die from a drug overdose that day. In fact, around 200 Americans die from an overdose every day, while each day an estimated 3,600 kids under 18 try an illicit drug for the first time.

We created the Victoria's Voice Foundation and devote our time shining a bright light on this dark issue. Through the foundation, our family is bringing the issue of drugs to the national stage and championing ways to reduce drug experimentation, addiction, and overdose. Our goal is to change the reality of drug addiction in the United States.

The Victoria's Voice Foundation supports:

- Legislation that encourages people to use a lockbox for prescription medications because 53 percent of kids who use illicit prescription drugs get them from a relative's or friend's medicine cabinet.

- Legislation that would require a co-prescription of the opiate-reversal drug naloxone every time an opioid prescription is given. Naloxone can pull someone out of an overdose into immediate withdrawal, even if the person is on the verge of death.

- Having every first responder and university and college carry doses of the lifesaving and nonaddictive antidote naloxone.

- The implementation of a policy platform for random drug testing in partnership with educational institutions.

Our foundation played a pivotal role in Congress passing the Comprehensive Addiction and Recovery Act.

The Victoria's Voice Foundation also speaks to organizations about how families can discourage drug experimentation among kids, how to lower the likelihood their children will abuse drugs or become addicted, and how to avoid accidental overdose.

To learn more, visit **VictoriaSiegelFoundation.org**.

Our singular mission is saving lives so we don't lose our future generations to drug abuse and addiction.

About Jackie Siegel

Jackie Siegel is best known for her role in the award-winning documentary feature, *The Queen of Versailles* (Magnolia Pictures), which premiered at the Sundance Film Festival in 2012 and continues to be one of the most popular movies on Netflix. The documentary was included on Vogue's list of 66 Best Documentaries of All Time. In early 2018, Jackie was featured in the follow-up documentary, *Generation Wealth*.

Jackie earned the "Queen" moniker a decade ago, when she and husband, David Siegel, began an extravagant project to build the largest private residence in the United States—named Versailles—and the ambitious construction ground to a halt as the '08 recession dented their fortune. The rise and fall of their grand ambitions were captured in the critically acclaimed 2012 documentary based on their plans for the 90,000-square-foot behemoth near Orlando, FL. Currently on track for completion next fall, there's rumor the French original may look modest by comparison to the Siegel's version with 10 kitchens, an ice skating rink, and a 5,000-square-foot closet.

As an intriguing fixture in pop culture, Jackie has made

headlines with mainstream media (including *Us Weekly* and *People* magazine). She has appeared on hit television shows like Bravo's *Flipping Out* and *Watch What Happens Live with Andy Cohen*.

Philanthropy is a cause Jackie holds dear to her heart, which fueled her energy to create a charity of her own two years ago, the Victoria's Voice Foundation, in honor of her late daughter. She also is concerned with giving back to local communities and founded the Ocoee Thrift-Mart whose proceeds are donated to local non-profit organizations.

While Jackie has a full schedule as model, actress, and philanthropist, she is also a devoted wife to Westgate Resorts Founder and CEO David Siegel. Mrs. Siegel also sits on the Board of Directors for the Westgate Resorts Foundation. Jackie served as the host for Mrs. America 2018 at Westgate Las Vegas.

About David Siegel

David Siegel is the founder, CEO, and president of Westgate Resorts.

As a pioneer in the tourism industry, David has spent the past 30 years building CFI/Westgate Resorts into the largest privately owned company in Central Florida. David's empire includes timeshares, real estate, construction, hotel and apartment management, travel services, telecommunications, citrus, insurance, transportation, retail, and much more. David's success began in the 1970s when he purchased a prime piece of real estate that he later developed into the largest single site of vacation ownership in the world—Westgate Vacation Villas. David has been honored as the Entrepreneur of the Year for construction and real estate in Central Florida and finished second in the Entrepreneur of the Year national competition.

David studied marketing and management at the University of Miami. He also holds an honorary doctorate from Florida A&M University for his work in community service.

As chairman of the David A. Siegel Society (the Westgate Resorts Foundation's highest level of contributors), David has earned recognition as an outstanding and committed member of the Central Florida business community. David sits on the board of many civic organizations, including the board of directors for the Florida 2012 Olympics committee. He also has earned the National Community Service Award from the American Resort Development Association (ARDA).

Epilogue
by David Siegel

People are dying from ignorance. What I mean is parents don't know what to look for in their children. If their child has a drug problem, they don't recognize it. For example, when Victoria was growing up, I didn't know what to look for. I thought she was a typical teenager, moody from day to day. One day she was lovable, and the next day she hated me. To make sure she was okay, I sent her to a psychiatrist for counseling, and when she came home, she said he put her on Xanax. To me, that was like Advil. I didn't know the difference. Several months later she was still acting strange, so I sent her back to the psychiatrist. When she came home, I asked what happened, and she said that he increased her dosage.

I had no idea what she was doing. She covered up her arms, so I didn't see the scars on her wrists from when she tried to kill herself. I didn't see the body piercings or the tattoos. I now know almost every drug addict has body piercings, tattoos, and physical evidence of trying to harm themselves. Ignorance comes in many forms. One day Victoria came to me and said, "I've checked myself into rehab, and I'm trying to get off Xanax," and I said, "Wonderful, I'm glad you are doing something about it." She told the counselor that she was suicidal, but I was not told because she was 18. Six days later, she checked herself out of rehab, after meeting a young man there. I didn't know that you can't kick an addiction in less than 90 days. People go to rehab for 30 days, which is too short a time. It takes a minimum of 90 days to get over an addiction. In 30 days, all that happens is you are detoxed and counseled and then kicked out, usually when the insurance money runs out. Rehab programs typically cost $1,000 a day, and insurance companies pay for only 30 days. You are the most vulnerable after 30 days because you've been detoxed and counseled but haven't been cured. Then you fall off the wagon and start taking the same dose that you were taking when you went into rehab, but because you have been detoxed, your body can no longer tolerate the dose. More people die right after detox than at any other time.

Naloxone (Narcan)

When Victoria overdosed and the first responders were called, they did not carry naloxone. Very few people four years ago—and even today—know what naloxone is. I certainly didn't. Naloxone was invented in 1971, and if administered in time after an opioid overdose, it can save lives. It also goes by the name Narcan, which is the trademark. Today most law enforcement officers and first responders carry it. It is FDA approved and 100 percent safe. If it is given to someone who is sleeping or unconscious for any reason other than opioid overdose, it will have no effect on them. It only affects opioids. When you take opioids, they go to the receptors in your brain that control your breathing. When you have opioids in your system, they coat the receptors and cause your breathing to slow down or stop. Naloxone cleans off those receptors, and you start breathing again. After being administered naloxone, you have only

90 minutes to get to an emergency room and begin detoxing because you still have the opioids in your system, and after the 90
minutes they start coating the receptors again. You would have to
continue to give the person naloxone every 90 minutes to prevent
the receptors from getting coated again. It is also called the Lazarus
drug because it brings people back from the brink of death.

Marijuana

Another way that we are ignorant about the drug epidemic is that
few people know that marijuana is the gateway drug to cocaine and
heroin and yet many states have not only legalized medical marijuana but also recreational marijuana. In the past four years, I have
visited many rehabs and I have listened to hundreds of addicts tell
their life stories. Every single one of them without exception started
experimenting with marijuana when they were 14 or 15 years old.
Most of them were heroin addicts. Occasionally people who had a
sports injury, a major surgery, or even just a wisdom tooth pulled
were prescribed painkillers and became addicted. But the majority
of them started in middle school with marijuana. Nobody starts
with heroin. When people experiment with marijuana, they get a
high, but after a while, the body gets used to it and they have to take
more and more to get the same high. Finally, when the craving becomes so strong, they go to stronger drugs like cocaine and heroin
and also prescription drugs, which are more expensive than heroin
and cocaine. If you gathered all the people who need medical marijuana, they wouldn't be enough to sustain an industry. The pot
shops are counting on kids using it. Medical marijuana is for people
who have epilepsy, seizures, or terminal cancer. There is a product
made from marijuana, called Charlotte's Web, that has very low
THC, which is the chemical in marijuana that makes you high.

Drug Testing

Today there are 25 million people who are using drugs just to get high, and there are another 25 million former drug users who are in recovery. You must not have used drugs for five years to be considered in recovery. That's 50 million people, and with their parents alone, not counting brothers, sisters, cousins, aunts, and uncles, nearly half our population is affected by drugs. The only way to stop more people from getting into the pipeline is by instituting drug testing in our middle schools. The fear of getting caught is the best deterrent against starting. It's the best way to get somebody to stop if they already started, and it's the best defense against peer pressure. When their friend says, "Smoke a joint with me so you can be cool like me," they can say, "I'm as cool as you, but I'm afraid I'll get caught." In Central Florida there are five private schools that all have drug testing, and all are considered drug-free. Yet in every public school, you can go down the hallways and buy any drug you want. Why should children—usually from affluent families—who go to private schools be drug-free, but the majority of the kids who go to public schools are subject to drugs?

Pandemic

I used to think that drug addicts lived under bridges and slept on park benches, but I now know that the more affluent the family is the greater chance they have of having a child with a drug problem. Every day 200 people—mostly our future generation—die from drug overdoses, and you don't hear a whimper about it. If an airliner crashed with 200 people on board, it would be all over the news. Yet no strong action is being taken; it is a worse crisis than Russia, North Korea, China, Iran, and ISIS. They are not our major problem—the drug epidemic is. Every year more people have died from a drug overdose than all those who died in the Vietnam War. There's a stigma surrounding drug addiction, and families are ashamed to talk about it. It's time we did something about it. The United States is the only country in the world where life expectancy is going down because of the drug epidemic.

Prescriptions

The United States has 5 percent of the world's population but issues 90 percent of the world's prescription drugs. Doctors don't know how to prescribe. They get only a few hours of training in medical school and are usually taught how to prescribe a drug by the drug company's representatives. Fortunately, Florida and some other states are limiting the number of prescriptions that doctors can issue.

When people have leftover medications, they store them on the bathroom counter or in their medicine cabinets, but this gives their kids and their friends access to them. There are even cases where people who have a house for sale and have an open house have some people come in not to buy but to steal their prescriptions. Leftover medications should not be flushed down the toilet because they get into the water system. People need to lock up their prescriptions. We are losing our future generations of entrepreneurs like Bill Gates and Steve Jobs, the cure for cancer, music you will never hear, movies you will never see, and books you will never read. It's vital we take action and do something by ending this pandemic now. Your children and your grandchildren are dependent on you. Become as knowledgeable as you can about this problem. Ignorance is no longer an excuse. Ignorance can cost you your child's life. It cost me mine.

Acknowledgments

We'd like to thank our friends and family who supported us through the most difficult time of our lives and encouraged the publication of this book.

We'd also like to thank everyone at the Victoria's Voice Foundation for working so tirelessly to change the reality of drug addiction in the United States.

Finally, thank you to the team at Momosa Publishing, especially CEO Jennifer Bright Reich, writer Marie Suszynski, designer Joanna Williams, cover designer Leanne Coppola, and copy editor Amy Kovalski.

How You Can Help

You can make a difference. Donate your money and give your time to organizations that prevent drug abuse.

We are gathering stories of families that have been impacted by drugs. Share your story at **www.victoriasvoicebook.com** or **http://momosapublishing.com/share-your-story**.

We hope to gather these stories into a book to inform and inspire families and protect all of our children from drug abuse.

Connect with us!

f TheRealQueenofVersailles
www.victoriasvoicebook.com
contact@victoriasvoicebook.com

Peace Out